HISTORIC BRITAIN

FROM THE AIR

HISTORIC BRITAIN

FROM THE AIR

NICHOLAS BEST

PHOTOGRAPHY BY JASON HAWKES

PHOENIX ILLUSTRATED

Contents

Acknowledgements
7

Introduction
8

Chapter One
Southeast England
12

Chapter Two
The South and West
46

Chapter Three
London
74

Chapter Four
East Anglia
82

Chapter Five
The West Midlands
90

Chapter Six
North from the Thames Valley
104

Chapter Seven
The North Midlands
116

Chapter Eight
Wales
126

Chapter Nine
The North
138

Chapter Ten
Scotland
148

Index
160

THE AUTHOR

Nicholas Best was educated at the King's School, Canterbury, where he first acquired his love of historic buildings. After graduating from Trinity College, Dublin, he became a historian and author. He has written *Happy Valley*, the story of the English in Kenya, and two novels. He lives in Cambridge, in a listed building on the site of a manor house mentioned in the Domesday Book.

THE PHOTOGRAPHER

Jason Hawkes and his partner and pilot Tim Kendall have been taking photographs from the air for many years. They have produced aerial photographs for a number of highly successful books, among them *London from the Air*, *Country Houses from the Air*, *Provence* (with Peter Mayle), *Scotland from the Air* and *Ireland from the Air*.

Text © Nicholas Best, 1995
Photographs © Jason Hawkes, 1995

First published in 1995 by George Weidenfeld & Nicolson Ltd

This paperback edition first published in 1997 by Phoenix Illustrated
Orion Publishing Group, Orion House
5, Upper St Martin's Lane
London WC2H 9EA

British Library Cataloguing-in-Publication Data
A catalogue record for this book is available from
the British Library

ISBN 0-75380-217-1

Edited by Lucas Dietrich
Designed by Bradbury and Williams
Designer: Bob Burroughs
Printed and bound in Italy

All images are available to license from the Jason Hawkes Library at www.jasonhawkes.com

BIBLIOGRAPHY

Blue Guide to Wales, A and C Black, 1990
Paul Johnson, *Cathedrals of England, Scotland and Wales*, Weidenfeld & Nicolson, 1990
Paul Johnson, *London from the Air*, Holt, Rhinehart and Winston, 1984
Annabel Walker, *England from the Air*, Harry N. Abrams, 1989
Christopher Stanley, *The History of Britain – An Aerial View*, Batsford, 1984
Anna Sproule and Michael Pollard, *The Country House Guide*, Century, 1988
Ed. John Hadfield, *The Shell Guide to England*, Michael Joseph, 1981
The Country Life Book of Castles and Houses in Britain, Country Life Books, 1986
Sibylla Jane Flower, *Debrett's The Stately Homes of Britain*, Webb and Bower, 1982
Daniel P. Mannix, *The Hell-Fire Club*, New English Library, 1970
Adrian Tinniswood, *Country Houses from the Air*, Weidenfeld & Nicolson, 1994
Francis Thompson, *Shell Guide to Northern Scotland and the Islands*, Michael Joseph, 1987
Roy Mackal, *The Monsters of Loch Ness*, Macdonald and Jane's, 1976
Peter Howell and Elizabeth Beazley, *The Companion Guide to South Wales*, Collins, 1977
John Hilling, *Snowdonia and North Wales*, Batsford, 1980
George Mott, *Follies and Pleasure Pavilions*, Pavilion 1989
Alec Clifton-Taylor, *Buildings of Delight*, Gollancz, 1986
Gwyn Headley and Wim Meulenkamp, *Follies*, Cape, 1986
Ed. Mark Amory, *The Letters of Evelyn Waugh*, Weidenfeld & Nicolson, 1980

COVER PHOTOGRAPHS

Front cover: Arundel Castle, West Sussex.
Back cover: Bodiam Castle, Kent.

DEDICATION
Remembering Douglas Bell, of the Blackethouse Bells
N.B.

To my mother, Gillian (have you had your second cup?) Hatch
With much love, Jason

ACKNOWLEDGEMENTS
With thanks to Bill and Sue Mason, the Duke of Rutland and Sir Francis Dashwood
N.B.

ENDPAPERS: WESTBURY WHITE HORSE,
WILTSHIRE
PAGE 1: HMS VICTORY, PORTSMOUTH, HAMPSHIRE
PAGE 2: SISSINGHURST, KENT
PAGE 4: CLIVEDEN, BUCKINGHAMSHIRE
PAGE 7: IGTHAM MOTE, KENT

INTRODUCTION

 he British have one priceless advantage over most other countries in Europe – they have not had a foreign army on their soil for very nearly a thousand years. No enemy troops have rampaged unchecked through their towns and villages, stealing everything they could lay their hands on, burning everything they could not. No generals have waged war on the countryside, ordering the wholesale destruction of anything that might be of comfort to the inhabitants. No armies have turned their artillery on city after city, hammering away until nothing of any value is left. To be sure, there have been civil wars. To be sure, the English have wreaked havoc in Scotland and Wales. To be sure, the *Luftwaffe* did its best to flatten some of the country's most beautiful cities during the last war. But the damage, by comparison with most of Europe, has been negligible to say the least. The fabric of the country over the past thousand years has suffered far more from neglect or property development than from the ravages of fire and sword, bomb and bullet.

'AS A DIRECT CONSEQUENCE, THE BRITISH ISLES ARE BLESSED WITH A WEALTH OF ANCIENT BUILDINGS FROM EVERY STAGE OF THEIR DEVELOPMENT'

As a direct consequence, the British Isles are blessed with a wealth of ancient buildings from every stage of their development – a historical record as rich and diverse as any in the world. Most of these buildings date, inevitably, from after the Norman conquest, but many are much earlier. From Stonehenge onwards, every generation has left its mark, some more permanently than others. There is still plenty to see from the Iron Age, for instance, from the stone-built brochs along the Scottish coast to the hilltop forts of middle England to the village settlements of Devon and Cornwall. Plenty to see from the Roman occupation too – villas, forts, bathhouses, any number of forums and basilicas, all of them still there, just below the surface of the earth. The Romans built to last and some of what they built – the walls of Portchester Castle are an obvious example – still stands to its full height, nearly 2000 years later.

Rather less remains from the Dark Ages, largely because the Vikings and Anglo-Saxons preferred to build with wood, which was cheaper and in abundant

ALTHOUGH ONLY USED BY PEDESTRIANS NOW, IRONBRIDGE, ON THE RIVER SEVERN, WAS A MASTERPIECE OF TECHNOLOGY IN ITS TIME. IT IS A MONUMENT TO THE INDUSTRIAL REVOLUTION, THE FIRST BRIDGE EVER CONSTRUCTED OF CAST IRON. FOUNDATIONS WERE LAID IN 1769 AND THE BRIDGE OPENED TO TRAFFIC 10 YEARS LATER.

supply. A few bits of masonry have been incorporated into the walls of later monastic developments, and a few Saxon churches still exist – indeed are still in use. By and large though, most of what was built between the Romans and the Normans has long since rotted away, destroyed by Britain's dank and cheerless climate. It was not until the Normans invaded in 1066 that buildings began to be erected again of any lasting significance.

The Normans were great builders, particularly of castles and cathedrals. Their first castles were of wood, hastily improvised from the surrounding forests. As soon as possible though, they built more permanent structures of stone, often importing their materials from France for the purpose. They built cathedrals too, of which the most outstanding example is Durham, on a horseshoe bend on the river Wear. There is no finer Norman building anywhere in Europe. Largely unaltered since its completion in 1133, the cathedral is so well constructed that it still looks as if the architects have only popped out for five minutes and will be back again at any moment.

'THE NORMANS WERE GREAT BUILDERS, PARTICULARLY OF CASTLES AND CATHEDRALS.'

The Middle Ages saw a continuation of the process, a development of the Normans' grand designs. Castles were greatly expanded and embellished, cathedrals developed into the magnificent creations that still dominate most of Britain's older cities. The best of them – and there is a wide choice – were works of art in their own right, works that have never subsequently been equalled, let alone bettered. The cathedrals employed a whole range of mediaeval craftsmen to sustain them, men brought in from as far away as France and Italy, bringing with them building and artistic skills that were the best in the business.

The Middle Ages saw the first flowering also of the English stately home – a revolutionary idea at the time, whereby the castle of old ceased to be a place of defence, bristling with fortifications, and became instead a place of repose, somewhere for grand families to be at ease and take their leisure. The idea was enthusiastically adopted by the Tudors, taking advantage of more settled times to build lavish country houses for themselves, many of which are still standing today, still occupied by the same families. But the idea achieved its full bloom perhaps in the grand classical designs of the 18th and 19th centuries, the Baroque and Palladian mansions – Stourhead, Ickworth, Castle Howard – so beloved of the British aristocracy. Other European countries have built stately homes as well, yet nowhere has the art form taken so deep a hold as in Britain.

Mention should also be made of the many lesser buildings which survive from earlier times: the mediaeval churches, thousands of them, at the heart of so many villages; the manor houses and rectories; the guildhalls and workmen's cottages, none of them particularly grand, yet as much a part of the historical record as anywhere else. And of course the eccentricities – the follies of all shapes and sizes, the black and white timbered houses so crazily built that they seem ready to topple over, the odd-looking towers that appear to have no discernible purpose whatsoever. It's a catalogue as diverse and eclectic, as richly inventive, as any in the world.

But why from the air? For all sorts of good reasons, yet chiefly perhaps because an aerial view does very definitely provide a different perspective on the subject. Take St Paul's cathedral for instance, Sir Christopher Wren's masterpiece in the heart of London. It is splendidly imposing form the ground, but a ground view gives no hint at all of the immense false walls concealing the buttresses behind. Wren was a master at that kind of deceptive architecture, yet it is only from the air that his real genius becomes apparent.

'ALL OF THEM PHOTOGRAPH PERFECTLY WELL FROM THE GROUND, YET IT IS ONLY FROM THE AIR THAT ONE CAN SEE THEM IN CONTEXT, FORM AN IMPRESSION OF HOW THEY FIT INTO THEIR OFTEN COMPLEX SURROUNDINGS.'

Take Stirling Castle too, or the dual castles at Sherborne, at one of which Sir Walter Ralegh was famously doused with ale by an over-zealous servant. Or Eton, Salisbury or the Clifton suspension bridge over the river Avon. Or Brightling churchyard, with its extraordinary pyramid tomb, or Chartwell, where Sir Winston Churchill lived for more than 40 years. All of them photograph perfectly well from the ground, yet it is only from the air that one can see them in context, form an impression of how they fit into their often complex surroundings.

The idea is not new. Aerial views have been around for several hundred years, imaginatively depicted by artists who themselves had both feet firmly planted on the ground. Comparing their work to a later photograph, it is amazing how accurate they managed to be, with only their intuition to guide them. When all is said and done however, there is really no substitute for the real thing, a couple of men in a helicopter: one to take the pictures, the other to provide the best possible platform for the shot. Jason Hawkes and his pilot Tim Kendall are among the best aerial photographers in the business. Here is a collection of their pictures to prove it.

CHAPTER ONE

SOUTHEAST ENGLAND

THE INVASION COAST

obody knows for sure where Julius Caesar first set foot in Britain in 55 BC, but all the evidence points to the Kentish coast, on the gently shelving beach between Walmer and Deal. His first choice was Dover, whose legendary white cliffs were clearly visible to the Roman soldiers massing across the Channel. But the cliffs were so sheer, and the warriors on top of them so menacing, that Caesar thought better of it and turned to the north instead. Seven miles beyond Dover, closely shadowed by the English on shore, he anchored off the beach and launched his troops towards the shallows. The first serious invasion of Britain had begun.

It was no pushover for the Romans. The English resisted fiercely. Wild, long-haired, covered in woad to frighten their enemies, they were not the kind of men to give in without a fight. A strong force of them plunged into the shallows and advanced towards the Romans to stop the invaders getting ashore. The battle that followed was fast and furious. For a while it looked as if the Romans would never leave the safety of their ships and would be forced to abandon the invasion. But then the eagle bearer of the 10th Legion – with more courage, one suspects, than brains – jumped overboard and headed for the beach, determined that nothing was going to stop him. His comrades followed, the English withdrew, and the rest, as they say, is history.

'THE BATTLE OF HASTINGS LASTED ALL DAY AND VERY NEARLY ENDED IN DEFEAT FOR WILLIAM THE CONQUEROR.'

And, as history tends to, it repeated itself, though not in precisely the same form, and not for more than a thousand years. It wasn't until 1066 that the British mainland was successfully invaded again – give or take a few Viking raids. The landing this time was at Pevensey Bay, a few miles along the Sussex coast from Hastings. Here again the invaders came from France; here again the natives resisted fiercely. The Battle of Hastings lasted all day and very nearly ended in defeat for William the Conqueror. He swore to his Norman knights that he would build a church on the site if God would only grant him victory – and was as good as his word. The high altar was erected on the spot where King Harold is believed

ON A SPUR OVERLOOKING THE RIVER, ARUNDEL CASTLE WAS BUILT TO DEFEND THE SUSSEX HINTERLAND AGAINST FRENCH INVASION.

to have been killed by an arrow in the eye, and the place is still marked by a commemorative stone today.

Harold's death is usually taken as the starting point of modern British history, ushering in as it did a period of strong government and continuing stability that has lasted – with a few hiccups – for almost a thousand years. But if no foreign army has ever invaded Britain since the Norman Conquest, it is certainly not for want of trying. Almost the first thing William did after his victory was to erect a wooden fort at Hastings and another at Dover, a precursor of the stone castle that stands there today. William knew the importance of defence, and his successors were quick to follow his lead.

In the centuries that followed the Norman invasion, an elaborate chain of defences was established along the coasts of Kent, Sussex and Hampshire. It included strongpoints of all shapes and sizes, everything from Norman castles and Tudor forts to Spanish Armada beacons, Martello towers of the Napoleonic era, pillboxes and gun emplacements from 1940. Most of the defences are still standing, mute testimony to 900 years of fear and insecurity, 900 years of British distrust of the sea and what it might bring. Few other coastlines in the world have been as heavily protected in the past as that of southeast England. Few have ever needed to be.

Inland too it was much the same story, at least to begin with. The Normans' first priority was to consolidate their hold on their new territory. They did so by building castles as soon as they could, great stone fortresses that could withstand long sieges and serve as a rallying point for the defence of the area. The castles took a long time to complete – hundreds of years, usually, by the time they had been added to and refined – but the results were spectacular, to say the least. There can be few more beautiful castles in the world than Leeds, near Maidstone; few grander than Arundel, in Sussex; few more intriguing than Hever in Kent, where the window from which Anne Boleyn first set eyes on Henry VIII can still be seen. Some castles are in ruins now, but most are still inhabited, a few even remaining in the hands of the original families, who can trace their ancestry back to the robber barons of five, six hundred years ago and occasionally even longer.

But castles were expensive and not every important family – whether Norman or, increasingly, English – could afford one. For those who couldn't, a fortified manor house was often the next best thing. Indeed manor houses became the norm after gunpowder rendered heavier fortifications obsolete. Scotney Castle, at Lamberhurst, is really little more than a fortified manor, its defences strengthened after a French attack in 1377 and dignified with the name of castle.

Together with Ightham Mote – one of very few manors to retain the original moat – it must be one of the prettiest houses of its type in England. Sissinghurst Castle too is very pretty, although really only a manor house. More formidable than any of them are Penshurst Place and Knole, both of which began as large country houses and then expanded to become virtually palatial in scope.

For ordinary people though, the safest bet in troubled times was to cluster together in villages and towns, preferably in the lee of a castle or else surrounded by a good stout wall to keep invaders out. A prime example is Canterbury, which boasts a Roman city wall and a Norman castle, as well as a magnificent cathedral – 'the noblest tower in Christendom'. Canterbury boasts other attractions as well, because after the murder of Thomas à Becket in 1170, it became the third most important place of pilgrimage in the Christian world, rivalled only by Rome and Jerusalem. Even today, the site of the martyrdom is visited by almost two million people every year, looking very much as it did when Chaucer's pilgrims came to see it more than 600 years ago.

'FEW OTHER COASTLINES IN THE WORLD HAVE BEEN AS HEAVILY PROTECTED IN THE PAST AS THAT OF SOUTHEAST ENGLAND.'

Over the centuries however, the mood changed and violence ceased to be the rule in England. In time, the need for defence became less important as the country became more settled. The battle of Bosworth in 1485 put an end to a long period of disorder in British history, and the architecture of the next 150 years reflected the peace and prosperity that Henry VII and his successors brought to the land. The big houses of Tudor times were almost invariably built for show rather than defence, with much greater emphasis on gardening and less on fortification. So too were those of the early Stuarts.

There was unrest again under Charles I, but not for long, and since the 1640s no war of any kind has been fought on English soil. Buildings erected since then have always been the buildings of a people at peace with their neighbours. Villages such as Chilham and Chiddingstone in Kent, or Rye in Sussex (Henry James's home for many years), blossomed after the Restoration and have not altered much in the intervening three centuries. Westerham too (where the homes of William Pitt the Younger, General Wolfe and Sir Winston Churchill can be visited) is little changed from the 18th century.

So settled indeed has the country been for the past 300 years that for a long time it was even fashionable among landowners to build 'follies' on their estates - fake castles, such as Hadlow in Kent, designed for no other purpose than to draw the eye and improve the view. The mind boggles as to what Julius Caesar, or William the Conqueror, would have made of that.

SISSINGHURST CASTLE

Sissinghurst has a special place in English hearts, the sort of house everyone would like to live in if only they could afford it. The buildings date from the 15th and 16th centuries, but suffered many years of neglect. French prisoners were housed there during the Seven Years War, leaving the place in such a mess that it could only be used as a workhouse thereafter. It was a ruin by the time Harold Nicolson and his wife Vita Sackville-West bought it in 1930. They painstakingly restored the buildings and established a beautiful garden, much of it laid out in Elizabethan style. The Nicolsons' descendants still live in the house, but the 16th century tower where Vita wrote her novels is open to the public.

PERHAPS THE BEST LOVED OF SISSINGHURST'S GARDENS IS THE WHITE GARDEN, DEVOTED TO SILVER-LEAFED WHITE-FLOWERING PLANTS, DIVIDED BY BOX HEDGES.

SCOTNEY CASTLE

erched daintily on an island in its own private moat, Scotney is not a castle at all in the strictest sense. It began life as a mediaeval manor house, although little of the original building now remains. In 1377, it belonged to Roger Ashburnham when the nearby towns of Rye and Winchelsea were attacked by the French. Alarmed, Ashburnham obtained Royal permission to fortify his property with a curtain wall and four circular towers, one of which still survives intact. But the French did not attack again and the threat receded in subsequent generations. The tower was roofed at a later date and the main structure rebuilt, with a deliberately romantic look. Today the castle remains, as it has always been, a private house.

THE GROUNDS AT SCOTNEY ARE LOVINGLY TENDED, ESPECIALLY THE 'ALPINE' GARDEN, PLANTED ON THE SIDE OF AN OLD QUARRY.

RYE

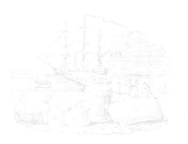

tanding at the mouth of the Rother, Rye was for centuries a thriving sea port. Though not one of the original members, it was later granted all the trading privileges of the Cinque Ports, in return for which it had to provide ships and sailors for the wars against France. The French themselves raided Rye at least four times, razing it to the ground in 1377. But times changed, and so did the landscape. Rye's harbour silted up in the 16th century and the sea receded almost two miles. Today the town is a tourist attraction, with mediaeval and Georgian houses and a wealth of cobbled streets. There is even an old smugglers' inn, complete with secret passages, which has changed little in centuries. Henry James lived in Rye for many years and wrote his later novels there.

IN THE MID-18TH CENTURY,
RYE WAS DOMINATED BY
THE HAWKHURST GANG, A
GROUP OF SMUGGLERS WHO
WERE OPENLY BOASTFUL OF
HOW THEY EARNED THEIR
LIVING.

IGHTHAM MOTE

pinion is divided as to whether Ightham takes its name from the surrounding moat or from the moot (council meeting) held there in the Middle Ages. What is certain however is that the original building, across the courtyard from the main entrance, dates from about 1340 and still has the original doorway, although the oriel window was put in later. The gatehouse tower was added in early Tudor times, and a barrel-vaulted ceiling in the chapel sports the roses of York, Lancaster and Tudor. It is thought the ceiling may have been taken from a temporary pavilion on the Field of the Cloth of Gold, where Henry VIII attempted to negotiate a European peace agreement with the French in 1520. Ightham has had a chequered career over the centuries and was in danger of demolition until its rescue in recent years.

IGHTHAM IS DOMINATED
NOW BY ITS TUDOR
GATEHOUSE, BUT THE
ORIGINAL PART OF THE
HOUSE ACROSS THE
COURTYARD IS MUCH OLDER.

ARUNDEL CASTLE

lthough in Sussex, Arundel belongs to the Duke of Norfolk and has been his ancestors' home for more than 700 years. It was the scene of a great conspiracy in 1397, when the Earl of Arundel plotted with the Duke of Gloucester and Archbishop of Canterbury to dethrone Richard II and murder the lords of the council. The original castle was largely destroyed by a Parliamentary siege in 1644 – the only Norman parts remaining are the keep and barbican, where the damage from Roundhead cannonballs is still visible above the archway. The rest of the castle was remodelled in the 19th century. The Norfolk family (Fitzalans and Howards) are leading Roman Catholics and have featured often in British history, most tragically with Catherine Howard, Henry VIII's fifth wife, who was executed at the age of 20 – for flirting.

DURING THE CIVIL WAR, THE ROUNDHEADS MOUNTED CANNONS ON TOP OF THE NEARBY CHURCH TOWER, SO THAT THEY COULD FIRE OVER THE CASTLE WALLS.

BATTLE ABBEY

In the heat of the Battle of Hastings, William of Normandy promised to build a church on the site if God would only grant him victory. God did, and William built the church on the spot where King Harold was killed. Little remains of it today, but the Benedictine abbey erected on firmer ground at the edge of the battlefield still stands, with the town of Battle in the background. The abbey was fortified in the 14th century, when the massive gateway was constructed. It was surrendered to Henry VIII in 1538, who in turn gave it to the Master of the Horse, Sir Anthony Browne. There was talk of Elizabeth I living there for a while, but this came to nothing. In subsequent years the abbey has seen a variety of uses, most recently as a girls' school.

THE ABBEY WAS MILDLY DAMAGED BY GERMAN BOMBS DURING THE WAR, BUT HAS SINCE BEEN RESTORED.

'IN THE HEAT OF THE BATTLE OF HASTINGS, WILLIAM OF NORMANDY PROMISED TO BUILD A CHURCH ON THE SITE IF GOD WOULD ONLY GRANT HIM VICTORY. GOD DID, AND WILLIAM BUILT THE CHURCH ON THE SPOT WHERE KING HAROLD WAS KILLED.'

BODIAM CASTLE

 odiam stands on the river Rother and owes its origin to the French sacking of nearby Rye and Winchelsea in 1377. To discourage raids further inland, Richard II gave one of his generals, Sir Edward Dalyngrigge, a licence to crenellate Bodiam's manor house. But Sir Edward abandoned the house altogether and built instead one of the last mediaeval castles. With an eye to comfort as well as defence, he insisted on lavish private rooms for his family, as well as 33 fireplaces and at least 24 lavatories, built into the walls. Bodiam was slighted by the Parliamentarians in the Civil War and remained in ruins for hundreds of years, until restored by Lord Curzon in the 1920s.

ALTHOUGH A RUIN NOW, THE CASTLE WAS 'STATE OF THE ART' IN ITS TIME. IT EVEN HAD A PRIMITIVE FORM OF CENTRAL HEATING IN THE WALLS.

'TO DISCOURAGE RAIDS FURTHER INLAND, RICHARD II GAVE ONE OF HIS GENERALS, SIR EDWARD DALYNGRIGGE, A LICENCE TO CRENELLATE BODIAM'S MANOR HOUSE.'

BRIGHTLING CHURCHYARD

ost people prefer to be buried lying down, but not 'Mad Jack' Fuller. Very rich and eccentric, he sat in the House of Commons for many years, despite being forcibly removed in 1810 for insulting the Speaker. He spent a fortune on gambling, regularly drank three bottles of port a day, and once proposed marriage to Susan Thrale, daughter of Dr Johnson's friend. When she refused him, he arranged for her to be followed everywhere by prostitutes from Tunbridge Wells. Fuller died in 1834 and was buried, as he had wished, in a pyramid in the churchyard on his estate. It is said that he sits there to this day, bolt upright in an iron chair, with a roast chicken and a bottle of port in front of him, waiting for the Resurrection. The floor of his tomb is strewn with pieces of broken glass, just in case the Devil in his cloven hooves arrives first.

STRICTLY SPEAKING, A PYRAMID IS A PAGAN DEVICE, WITH NO PLACE IN A CHRISTIAN CHURCHYARD. BUT FULLER WAS SQUIRE OF THE VILLAGE, SO HE COULD BE BURIED HOW HE LIKED.

BRIGHTON PAVILION

uilt on farmland close to the sea, the Royal Pavilion at Brighton is an oddity, to say the least. With an Indian exterior and a Chinese interior, it was designed as a holiday home for George IV, a little place in the country where he could relax with his mistresses and enjoy the sea air. Queen Victoria found it 'a strange, odd, Chinese-looking thing, both inside and out'. She preferred the Isle of Wight and was more than happy for the Pavilion to be taken over by the Brighton Corporation. The building lay semi-derelict for many years and served as a hospital during the First World War. It was only after the Second that enthusiasts restored it to its former glory. The Pavilion – a royal palace like no other – is a museum now, one of Brighton's main tourist attractions.

IT USED TO BE A FARMHOUSE IN THE MIDDLE OF THE COUNTRY, BUT NOW THE PAVILION FORMS THE CENTREPIECE OF A LARGE SEASIDE TOWN.

CHARTWELL

wo miles south of Westerham, in the Kentish weald, lies Chartwell, Sir Winston Churchill's home from 1922 until his death in 1965. The original farmhouse dates from the 17th century, but was greatly enlarged in Victorian times and again by Churchill, who added a new wing. He also redesigned the lake and built the wall of the vegetable garden with his own hands. Churchill spent a lot of time at Chartwell in the wilderness years before the Second World War, and again after he had retired from the premiership. The house is now a museum to his memory. Some rooms have been rearranged to accommodate the flow of visitors, but others remain exactly as they were when he used them. Particularly interesting is the study, decorated with mementoes from his extraordinary career.

'CHURCHILL SPENT A LOT OF TIME AT CHARTWELL IN THE WILDERNESS YEARS BEFORE THE SECOND WORLD WAR, AND AGAIN AFTER HE HAD RETIRED FROM THE PREMIERSHIP.'

CHURCHILL LIVED ALMOST HALF HIS LIFE AT CHARTWELL. HE BROUGHT UP HIS CHILDREN HERE AND ALSO ENTERTAINED MANY FAMOUS STATESMEN.

HADLOW CASTLE

heories abound as to why Hadlow Tower was built quite so tall. It stands 170 feet above the Kent countryside and was built between 1838 and 1848 for Walter Barton May, a wealthy local eccentric. 'May's folly' was originally an appendage to Hadlow Castle, but today it is the folly that survives while the castle has long since been demolished. May is supposed to have commissioned the tower after his wife left him, so that wherever she went in Kent, she wouldn't be able to forget him. It is said also that he wanted to see the ships on the Thames, forgetting that the Downs were in the way, or that after his death he wanted his corpse to be interred above ground, thus negating a prophecy that his family would lose the property after he was buried. Whatever the truth of the matter, the folly has indeed passed out of the family's hands, although it is still a private house, known today as Hadlow Castle.

THE FOLLY WAS INSPIRED BY A SIMILAR TOWER AT FONTHILL IN WILTSHIRE, WHICH HAD COLLAPSED IN 1825. THE ROYAL OBSERVER CORPS USED HADLOW AS A LOOKOUT POST DURING THE WAR.

HERSTMONCEUX
CASTLE

A red-brick castle somehow seems a contradiction in terms, but it is the only accurate description of Herstmonceux in Sussex. Built in the 15th century, with thin walls and slim turrets, the castle looks splendid enough but would never have stood up to a prolonged bombardment. It is a fortified manor house rather than a castle in the accepted sense of the word. The buildings were largely demolished in the 18th century, but restored again in the 1930s. In 1948 the Greenwich Observatory took them over and the castle became the official residence of the Astronomer Royal. The Isaac Newton telescope building was added in 1967. But Herstmonceux became a victim of Government cuts and now faces an uncertain future as hotel, golf club or perhaps even a university out-station.

OBSERVATORIES IN OTHER PARTS OF THE WORLD MAY ENJOY BETTER WEATHER, BUT NONE HAS A GRANDER SETTING THAN HERSTMONCEUX, IN THE HEART OF THE SUSSEX COUNTRYSIDE.

HEVER CASTLE

Hever looks splendid from the outside, but is really only a manor house fortified with a few turrets and dignified with the name of castle. It was the childhood home of Anne Boleyn, whose father Sir Thomas was England's ambassador to France. A window in the courtyard is popularly believed to be the one from which Anne first set eyes on Henry VIII.

The King had already seduced her sister, and wanted to seduce Anne too. But she held out for marriage or nothing. So Henry divorced his wife – incidentally separating the Church of England from Rome, dissolving the monasteries and setting the scene for more than a century of religious strife. Anne survived as Queen just long enough to give birth to the future Elizabeth I before losing her head for alleged adultery.

THE CASTLE HAS PASSED INTO THE HANDS OF BUSINESSMEN NOW, BUT THE GROUNDS ARE STILL USED FOR CULTURAL EVENTS.

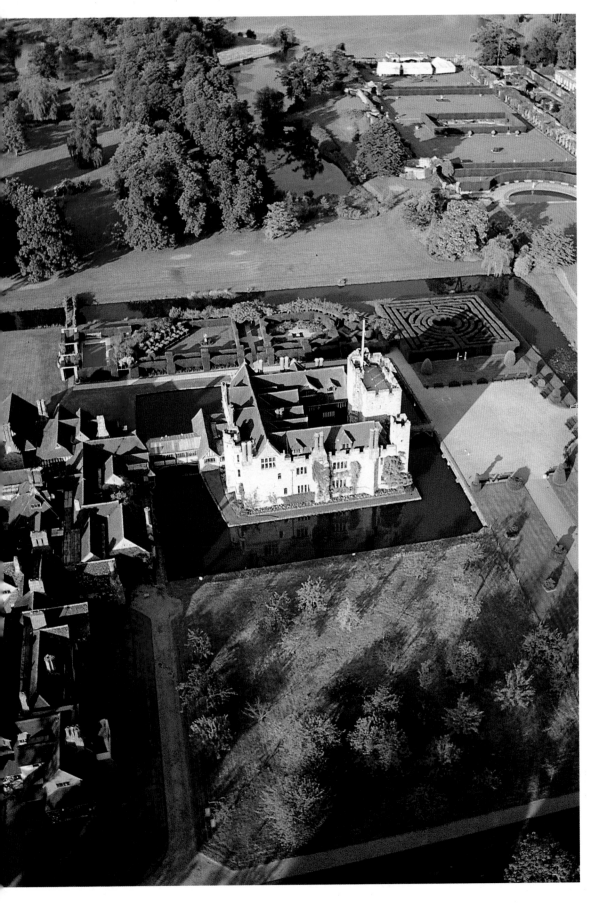

'A WINDOW IN THE
COURTYARD IS POPULARLY
BELIEVED TO BE THE ONE
FROM WHICH ANNE FIRST SET
EYES ON HENRY VIII.'

KNOLE

Few private houses come larger than Knole, in Kent, with seven courtyards, 52 staircases, and – it is thought – 365 rooms. The original mediaeval palace was greatly improved by Thomas Sackville, who became 1st Earl of Dorset in 1604. His descendants have lived there ever since, sometimes sumptuously, more often dreadfully short of money. One of the more outrageous owners was Charles Sackville, 6th Earl of Dorset, a Restoration rake and lover of Nell Gwynn (she always remembered him fondly as Charles the *first*). Another, two centuries later, was Lionel, 2nd Lord Sackville, who had seven illegitimate children by a Spanish dancer. Lionel's granddaughter, Vita Sackville-West, grew up at Knole and went on to enjoy many liaisons of her own, not least with Virginia Woolf, whose novel *Orlando* was an open love letter to Vita and the splendours of Knole.

KNOLE IS VAST ENOUGH TO BE A VILLAGE, RATHER THAN A PRIVATE HOUSE. THE OUTER COURTYARD (THE GREEN COURT) AND THE GATEHOUSE ALONG THE EAST FRONT WERE ADDED TO THE ORIGINAL BUILDING BY HENRY VIII.

TUNBRIDGE WELLS

arge and prosperous now, Tunbridge Wells wasn't even a clearing in the forest until 1606, when a passing aristocrat tasted the waters of the spring and decided they were good for his health. Lord North took a sample of the water back to London and spread the word among his friends. Soon a commercial enterprise had grown up and Tunbridge Wells was a very fashionable spa. The future Queen Anne visited in 1699, but was very annoyed when her son slipped and hurt himself on the mud by the spring. To placate her, the town council decided to pave the area around the wellhead with pantiles. The double row of 18th century buildings in the bottom half of the picture has been known as 'The Pantiles' ever since.

WILLIAM MAKEPEACE THACKERAY ONCE HAD A HOUSE ON TUNBRIDGE WELLS COMMON — THE HEIGHT OF MIDDLE CLASS GENTILITY, BOTH THEN AND NOW.

PENSHURST PLACE

Although it has been added to over the years, Penshurst remains at heart a 14th century manor house, one of the best preserved in the country. It was built for a Lord Mayor of London – a successful merchant, one of the first of his class to build on such a scale – but was later acquired by the Sidney family, who have lived there since 1552. The Elizabethan poet Sir Philip Sidney spent much of his childhood at Penshurst and it is believed that he based the house in *Arcadia* on his own home. Ben Jonson also sang Penshurst's praises, as did Edmund Waller and Robert Southey in later generations. Algernon Sidney, a committed republican, was buried there after being beheaded in 1683. The Baron's Hall, looking much as it did in the 14th century, is considered the finest of its kind in England.

PENSHURST WAS BUILT BY SIR JOHN PULTENEY, FOUR TIMES LORD MAYOR OF LONDON, WHO MADE A FORTUNE OUT OF WOOL BUT DIED OF THE BLACK DEATH IN 1349.

CHAPTER TWO

THE SOUTH AND WEST
HOME OF THE ROYAL NAVY

f southeast England is the invasion coast, then the south and west of the country can surely lay claim to being the home – for well over a millennium – of the Royal Navy. Blessed as it is by the waters of the Gulf Stream, blessed also by an abundance of creeks, inlets and deep water harbours, it was perhaps inevitable that the southwest should have developed a strong maritime tradition that began in the time of Alfred the Great and flourishes to this day.

Alfred was king of the West Saxons from 871 to 901 and is widely considered to have been the father of the Royal Navy. Other monarchs had toyed with the idea of a navy before, but he was first to put the idea into practice on a regular basis. In effect he was king of all the English, because his fellow rulers had all seen their kingdoms swept away by a prolonged series of invasions from Denmark and Norway. Alfred's response was to organise a fleet of ships to fight the invaders on the high seas before they had a chance to set foot ashore. The English knew little about sailing, so he hired his first crews in the Low Countries. From these slender origins, the Royal Navy developed over the centuries into a fighting force with a history as glorious as any navy's in the world.

Given the geography, it is hardly surprising that many of the great naval commanders grew up in the West country, or else had their bases there. The greatest commander of all, Lord Nelson, came from East Anglia, but he spent much of his home service in the southwest, and it was from Portsmouth in Hampshire that he set sail on his final voyage to the battle of Trafalgar. The royal dockyard at Portsmouth dates from 1194, and Nelson's flagship HMS *Victory* can still be visited there, the spot where he died clearly marked below decks.

Further along the coast, the other great naval base was and is at Plymouth, in Devon. Sir Walter Ralegh was a Devon man, as were Hawkins, Gilbert and Sir

'FROM THESE SLENDER ORIGINS, THE ROYAL NAVY DEVELOPED OVER THE CENTURIES INTO A FIGHTING FORCE WITH A HISTORY AS GLORIOUS AS ANY NAVY'S IN THE WORLD.'

THE BUILDING OF STONEHENGE WAS COMPLETED IN STAGES, FROM ABOUT 2200 BC TO 1300 BC. THE AXIS IS CAREFULLY ALIGNED WITH SUNRISE ON 21 JUNE, THE LONGEST DAY OF THE YEAR, WHICH SUGGESTS THAT IT WAS DESIGNED, AMONG OTHER THINGS, AS A GIGANTIC CALENDAR.

Francis Drake, who retired after his world voyage to Buckland Abbey, near Milton Combe. All of them used Plymouth as their base. Drake in particular is famous for continuing his game of bowls on Plymouth Hoe after news of the Spanish Armada had reached him. There is still a bowling green on the Hoe, not far from Drake's statue. In the harbour, a plaque commemorates the *Mayflower* steps, from where the Pilgrim Fathers are said to have departed for a new life in America.

This intrepid tradition is reflected in the fiction of the region as well. The West country has always been the setting for tremendous literary adventures, often with a maritime theme. Stevenson set the beginning of *Treasure Island* near Bristol, from where Long John Silver and his crew sailed away in the *Hispaniola*. Further along, Daphne du Maurier used the dramatic coastline of Cornwall as the backdrop for many of her books, notably *Frenchman's Creek* and *Jamaica Inn* (a real inn, still in business today, at Bolventor). Her own home – Menabilly, near Fowey – supplied the inspiration for Manderley in *Rebecca*, perhaps the greatest of all her novels.

'THE WEST COUNTRY HAS ALWAYS BEEN THE SETTING FOR TREMENDOUS LITERARY ADVENTURES, OFTEN WITH A MARITIME THEME.'

Thomas Hardy too is an author closely identified with the West country, although his native Dorset is sometimes considered to be in the South. He thought of himself as a 'Wessex' man first and foremost (claiming kinship, incidentally, with the Hardy who kissed Nelson at Trafalgar) and his novels are deeply imbued with the love he felt for his native turf. He was a master of the compelling image, never more striking perhaps than in the climax to *Tess of the d'Urbervilles*, when Tess and her husband flee towards Stonehenge after the murder of her lover. Hardy was fascinated by Stonehenge, by the sense of time and place it inspired, by the feeling of men shaped by the landscape, rather than the other way around. He was intrigued by the ancient history of the southwest: the Cerne Abbas giant (a huge fertility symbol cut into the chalk of a hillside), the Iron Age hill forts, the Bronze Age villages (such as Grimspound, in Devon). These, to him, were as much a part of Britain's heritage as the thatched cottages and stone manor houses of a later generation. His respect for the past found its way time and again into his work.

Other writers echoed his sentiments. Sir Arthur Conan Doyle was never a West countryman, but he did set one of the greatest of his Sherlock Holmes stories there. *The Hound of the Baskervilles* takes place almost entirely on Dartmoor, a bleak and windswept place, dominated then as now by prehistoric stone circles and a grim old prison housing some of the country's most dangerous criminals. R.D. Blackmore too caught something of the same atmosphere in *Lorna Doone*, his celebrated story of clan warfare on Exmoor at the time of the Bloody Assizes. And so did John Fowles in his novel *The French Lieutenant's Woman*, and other stories.

The French Lieutenant's Woman is actually set in Lyme Regis, on the Dorset coast, much of the action taking place around the 600-year-old harbour known as the Cobb. The Cobb has seen some real history as well, because it was in Lyme bay that the first skirmish took place between Drake and the Spanish Armada, in Lyme bay also that the Duke of Monmouth, illegitimate son of Charles II, landed to begin the ill-fated rebellion against his uncle, James II.

But it is as a seaside resort that Lyme Regis is best known – and has been since the 18th century. Jane Austen knew the town well, and loved it. She spent her holidays there from Chawton, in Hampshire, where she lived for a while in a cottage (still standing) on the estate of her brother. While at Chawton she wrote *Mansfield Park*, *Emma* and *Persuasion*, drawing heavily on her knowledge of the fashionable people she met in summer at Lyme Regis.

Jane Austen also lived in Bath at different times, and at Winchester, two of the loveliest towns of the southwest. So lovely indeed is Bath - little changed since her day – that it has achieved the rare distinction of being officially designated by the United Nations as a world heritage site. It owes its name to the Roman baths preserved near the abbey, but is better known as an almost perfect example of an 18th century town, the buildings in the centre all faced in stone of the same mellow honey colour.

'WINCHESTER ALSO BOASTS AN ANCIENT ROUND TABLE, WRONGLY ALLEGED TO HAVE BEEN THE ORIGINAL USED BY KING ARTHUR AND HIS KNIGHTS.'

Winchester too is an extraordinarily distinguished town. It is rather older than Bath, having been an important centre in Roman times and later the capital city for both Alfred the Great and William the Conqueror. Its most impressive buildings are mediaeval or earlier, notably the cathedral (where Jane Austen is buried, and also King Canute, whose failure to turn back the waves remains an object lesson in sound government), and the college, where the original school room has been in continuous use for over 600 years.

Winchester also boasts an ancient round table, wrongly alleged to have been the original used by King Arthur and his knights. It is displayed now on the wall of the assize court, where Sir Walter Ralegh was sentenced to death in 1603 for conspiring against James I. The sentence was delayed for many years and finally carried out at Westminster in 1618. Ralegh went bravely to his death, remarking that it didn't matter which way his head lay on the block, so long as his heart remained in the right place.

WHILE ON HOLIDAY AT
LYME, JANE AUSTEN IS SAID
TO HAVE FALLEN IN LOVE
WITH A MAN WHO LATER
PROVIDED THE MODEL FOR
CAPTAIN WENTWORTH IN
Persuasion.

LYME REGIS

Lyme Bay has been popular with holiday makers for hundreds of years – among them Jane Austen, who set her novel *Persuasion* there. But it has played its part in history as well, for it was in the bay, within sight of the shore, that the first skirmish took place in 1588 between the Spanish Armada and Sir Francis Drake's fleet (including five local ships). It was at Lyme Regis also that the Duke of Monmouth landed in 1685, to begin his ill-fated rebellion against his uncle James II. So many of his followers were subsequently exiled to the West Indies that to this day West Indians from certain islands speak with a pronounced West Country burr. Lyme's ancient harbour, The Cobb, was also the setting for John Fowles' novel *The French Lieutenant's Woman*, later filmed with Meryl Streep.

OSBORNE HOUSE

ormal and Italian-looking, Osborne was designed for Queen Victoria and Prince Albert as a holiday home on the Isle of Wight. Albert compared the sea view to the bay of Naples, which is a bit fanciful, but he and Victoria undoubtedly spent some of their happiest times there. They installed a life-size dolls' house in the grounds for their children, imported a Swiss chalet and built a miniature fort out of bricks fired by the young princes. After Albert's death, Victoria spent as much time as possible at Osborne, because of its happy memories, and died there herself in 1901. Many of the rooms today remain exactly as they were in Albert's time, notably the Durbar room, the Antler room and the Dining room with personalised miniature chairs for each of the Royal children.

MANY OF QUEEN
VICTORIA'S PETS ARE BURIED
ON OSBORNE'S TERRACES,
EACH WITH THEIR OWN
TOMBSTONE. DURING THE
SUMMER, SHE OFTEN ATE
BREAKFAST OUTSIDE — TO
THE SOUND OF BAGPIPES.

Bath

cross the square from Bath Abbey lie the Roman baths that gave the town its name. They remained hidden for centuries and were not seriously excavated until the 1870s. The baths themselves are original, but the surrounding columns are a 19th century reconstruction, very skilfully done. The water flowing through the system still uses some of the Roman pipes. Its therapeutic qualities have always been recognised, but it was not until the 18th century that Bath became a fashionable spa. Much of the best architecture dates from then, notably the Royal Crescent, the Pump Room, and the Pulteney Bridge over the Avon. This was designed by Robert Adam in the Florentine style, with shops all the way along, and has been popular with tourists as diverse as Jane Austen and Charles Dickens for more than 200 years.

The Pump Room, next to the Roman baths, was once frequented by Jane Austen.

BRADFORD-ON-AVON

radford is built on a hillside, a steep sloping town of narrow streets and ancient houses, many of them unchanged for centuries. It once belonged to the nuns of Shaftesbury, who used it as a haven against the Danes. It was a big cloth centre in the Middle Ages, which was why so many people could afford to build in the impressive local stone. Part of the bridge across the river dates from the 14th century, the rest from the 17th. An old chapel on the bridge was later converted into a small prison and now sits empty over the Avon. Further along, St Lawrence's church was built before the Norman Conquest, perhaps by St Aldhelm, but was somehow forgotten about in later centuries. It wasn't until 1856, when a vicar looked down over the rooftops and noticed an old cross, that the building's original purpose became apparent and it was restored to its proper function.

THE TOWN RISES SO STEEPLY FROM THE RIVER THAT PARTS OF IT HAVE TO BE STEPPED.

'Further along, St Lawrence's church was built before the Norman Conquest, perhaps by St Aldhelm, but was somehow forgotten about in later centuries.'

COWES

owes comes to life every August, when thousands of yachtsmen descend on it for one of the great social and sporting occasions of the year. Cowes Week has long enjoyed Royal patronage and in Edward Heath's time enjoyed Prime Minister's as well. The English first knew 1914 was going to be serious when Cowes Week was cancelled by the authorities. For the rest of the year however, Cowes is just a small town on the Isle of Wight, divided by the river Medina, with a regular ferry service across the Solent to Southampton on the mainland. Cowes Castle, now the Royal Yacht Squadron's headquarters on Victoria Parade, was built by Henry VIII in 1540 and served as the chief operations centre for the Normandy landings in 1944.

THE TOWN TAKES ITS NAME FROM TWO OLD FORTS, ONE LONG SINCE DEMOLISHED, GUARDING THE RIVER MOUTH LIKE A PAIR OF COWS. THE FIRST ENGLISH SETTLERS FOR MARYLAND SAILED FROM HERE IN 1633.

ST MICHAEL'S MOUNT

 Perched on a rocky outcrop off the Cornish coast, St Michael's is the ideal lookout post for an early warning of invasion. It was from the top of the church tower that the Spanish Armada was spotted in 1588 and a beacon lit to carry the news to the mainland. The island bears a startling resemblance to Mont St Michel, off the Brittany coast. It was for this reason that the monks of St Michel built a Benedictine priory on St Michael's shortly before the Norman Conquest. But the island made a better fortress than priory and the monks were evicted in 1425. The property passed from hand to hand before being sold to the St Aubyn family in 1657. They live there still, although the island belongs now to the National Trust.

DURING HIS ATTEMPT TO WREST THE THRONE FROM HENRY VII, PERKIN WARBECK LEFT HIS WIFE AT ST MICHAEL'S MOUNT FOR SAFEKEEPING. HENRY'S MEN ARRESTED HER THERE, AFTER WARBECK HAD SURRENDERED.

PORTCHESTER CASTLE

 ooking out over Portsmouth harbour, Portchester was built by the Romans in the 3rd century AD. The original wall of the fort is still standing, as are 14 of the bastions. The Saxons are thought to have captured the fort when they landed near Portsmouth in 501. Henry I added the keep at the beginning of the 12th century and built the moat around it. King John stayed at the castle when he was visiting Portsmouth, and Henry V used it as his base before setting sail for Agincourt. Henry VIII also stayed, with Anne Boleyn. But the castle passed out of royal hands in 1632 and fell into disrepair. It was used to house prisoners in the French and Dutch wars but now belongs to the Government and is open to the public.

UNUSUALLY, THE MOAT AT PORTCHESTER DOES NOT SURROUND THE WHOLE CASTLE, BUT ONLY THE 12TH CENTURY KEEP IN ONE CORNER.

NUNNEY CASTLE

ore a fortified house than a castle, Nunney was built in the French style by Sir John de la Mare, a soldier who had done well out of the Hundred Years War. Anxious to flaunt his new-found wealth, he obtained permission to crenellate (a mediaeval status symbol, the equivalent of a modern swimming pool) and completed the work in 1373. But the house was not designed for a serious attack, so it was a shock when Parliamentary forces besieged it in 1645. To show how well fed they were, the garrison tortured their only pig every day, as if it was being slaughtered. But the Parliamentarians didn't buy their act and Nunney fell – bad news for the garrison, yet even worse for the pig, which had been hoping for a prolonged siege.

THE CASTLE WAS SLIGHTED BY THE ROUNDHEADS AFTER THEY CAPTURED IT AND HAS LAIN DERELICT EVER SINCE.

LONGLEAT

ongleat is a product of its times, an immensely prosperous Tudor house – really a palace – built much more for show than defence. It began life as a 13th century priory, but was acquired by Sir John Thynne after the Dissolution of the Monasteries and has remained in the same family (now Marquesses of Bath) ever since.

Sir John rebuilt the house completely from the 1540s, and was still at it when he died in 1580. Elizabeth I was a guest at Longleat, as were Charles II and George II. But modern taxation has taken its toll – the family was forced to open Britain's first safari park in 1966. Seals now swim in the artificial lake and two gorillas live in the house on the island, where they greatly enjoy satellite TV.

THE GARDENS AT LONGLEAT, REMODELLED BY CAPABILITY BROWN IN THE 18TH CENTURY, CONTAIN SOME EXAMPLES OF HIS MOST IMPRESSIVE WORK.

FORDE ABBEY

orde Abbey dates from the 1140s, when it was built for an order of Cistercian monks. Unlike other such foundations, it acquired a good reputation for scholarship, but was still closed down by Henry VIII in 1539. Sir Edmund Prideaux bought it in 1649, shortly before becoming Oliver Cromwell's attorney-general. Unusually for the time, he chose to enlarge the property rather than rebuild,

gutting the interior and transforming it into an Italianate palace. The alterations were completed in 1660 and have changed little since. Prideaux's heir made the mistake of supporting the Duke of Monmouth's rebellion against James II, for which he was fined the then astronomical sum of £15,000. The estate has changed hands several times since then. It was once rented by Jeremy Bentham, who entertained his friend James Mill there.

IN THE 1900s, ODD NOISES WERE HEARD IN FORDE'S NORMAN CHAPEL — THE UNDERCROFT HAD FLOODED AND THE WOODEN COFFINS WERE BUMPING INTO EACH OTHER.

PLYMOUTH

orty years ago, Nikolaus Pevsner characterised Plymouth as 'the only British city whose existence appears to be centred on war'. Times have changed since then, but Plymouth is still a sailor's town, as it has been since the days of Drake and Ralegh. It was from the waters of Plymouth Sound that Drake sailed to attack the Spanish Armada, the Pilgrim Fathers sailed for America, and Charles Darwin set off round the world on the Beagle. William of Orange commissioned the royal dockyard on the marshland west of the town. Devonport, as the place became known, has been the home of the Royal Navy ever since. It can be seen above Brunel's railway bridge, which linked Devon to Cornwall in 1859. So important was the area to the British war effort that the Germans attacked Plymouth repeatedly from 1940 to 1943, flattening the centre and killing well over 1000 people in bombing raids.

ONCE 'A MENE THING AS AN INHABITATION FOR FISHERS', PLYMOUTH HAS LONG SINCE BLOSSOMED INTO A MAJOR INDUSTRIAL AND COMMERCIAL CENTRE.

SHERBORNE

herborne town boasts an abbey, a public school and two nearby castles, separated from each other by an artificial lake. The old castle, now a ruin, is Norman in origin. Sir Walter Ralegh tried to make a home there in the 1590s, but ended up building the new castle instead. It was at Sherborne that one of his servants, seeing him smoking a pipe and thinking he was on fire, doused him with a bucket of ale. After Ralegh's execution, the castle was given to the Digby family, who greatly expanded it. Anne Digby, Countess of Bristol, was living there during the Civil War when Parliamentary troops arrived with orders to raze it to the ground. Luckily, their commander was her brother, the Earl of Bedford, who backed off after she had given him a piece of her mind.

SURROUNDED BY THE
BUILDINGS OF THE PUBLIC
SCHOOL, SHERBORNE ABBEY
IS SO OLD THAT TWO SAXON
KINGS, ETHELBALD AND
ETHELBERT, WERE BURIED
THERE.

'THE HOUSE
IS ONE OF
ENGLAND'S
FIRST
PALLADIAN
MANSIONS,
COMPLETED
FOR THE
BANKER SIR
HENRY HOARE
IN 1725.'

STOURHEAD

 tourhead is a treasure, both for its house and its extensive grounds, brilliantly landscaped to an Italian design – 'one of the most picturesque scenes in the world', according to Horace Walpole. The house is one of England's first Palladian mansions, completed for the banker Sir Henry Hoare in 1725. Much of its furniture was designed by Thomas Chippendale the younger. Edward Gibbon browsed through the library at the age of 14 and is said to have been inspired by it to write the *Decline and Fall of the Roman Empire*. Stourhead's gardens were laid out from the 1740s by Sir Henry Hoare's son. Dotted around the lake are grottoes, a Temple of Flora, a Temple of the Sun, and a Pantheon copied from Rome. Alfred's Tower, in a corner of the estate, stands 160 feet high. It was built in 1772 on the spot where King Alfred is said to have raised his standard against the Danes in 878.

NO BOOK OF ENGLISH GARDENS IS COMPLETE WITHOUT A PICTURE OF STOURHEAD. THE GROTTO IS DECORATED WITH COUPLETS SPECIALLY COMPOSED FOR IT BY ALEXANDER POPE.

TAUNTON

Dominated by the tower of St Mary Magdalene church, Taunton is the county town of Somerset and has been an important trading centre for at least a thousand years, with a weekly market that pre-dates the Norman Conquest. To win its support against Matilda, King Stephen granted the town considerable privileges during the unrest of the 1140s, and Taunton has never looked back. It built the West country's first cloth-fulling mill in 1219 and remained at the heart of the wool industry for the next 500 years. The castle, originally 12th to 14th century, was largely rebuilt in 1496, then dismantled again at the Restoration, when its moat was filled in. Judge Jeffreys held one of his bloodier assizes there in 1685, punishing the many townspeople who had supported the Duke of Monmouth's rebellion against James II.

IT WAS AT TAUNTON THAT PERKIN WARBECK, CLAIMING TO BE ONE OF THE PRINCES IN THE TOWER, MADE A FULL CONFESSION TO HENRY VII AFTER HIS CAPTURE.

SALISBURY CATHEDRAL

Salisbury is surely one of the most beautiful cathedrals in the country. It traces its origins to the 13th century, when the Bishop of Sherborne decided to move his see from Old Sarum, a couple of miles away on a windy, waterless hill. The old cathedral was demolished (its foundations are still there) and a new one built on the present site. Legend has it that the actual spot was chosen by an arrow, fired at random. A clock in the north transept, dating from 1386, is the oldest in England. Henry Fielding, author of *Tom Jones*, lived in the cathedral close, as do several contemporary authors and one former Prime Minister, Edward Heath. Salisbury is rich in literary associations, for it was a trip around the cloisters, one summer evening, that inspired Trollope to write *The Warden* and *Barchester Towers*.

MOST UNUSUALLY FOR A CATHEDRAL TOWN, SALISBURY'S STREETS ARE LAID OUT ON THE AMERICAN GRID SYSTEM, RATHER THAN WINDING WHEREVER CHANCE TAKES THEM. THE CATHEDRAL SHOWS EARLY ENGLISH ARCHITECTURE AT ITS MOST SPLENDID.

CHAPTER THREE

LONDON
THE NATION'S CAPITAL

everal years ago, a Hollywood film featured a number of scenes set in London. Across the middle of the screen, the word 'London' appeared in large white letters, accompanied by an establishing shot of what appeared at first glance to be a fine mediaeval gateway. On closer inspection however, it turned out to be the entrance to Canterbury cathedral.

Yet the image counts for more than the reality, particularly in the film business. Even today, there are still people who think of London as at least in part a mediaeval city, with a wealth of ancient buildings and rows of tightly-packed slums, of the kind Dickens knew. Their perceptions are shaped by old Hollywood films, by dimly remembered extracts from *Oliver Twist* and *David Copperfield*, or the stories of Sherlock Holmes. But the reality, as anyone who has visited the modern office block at 221B Baker Street will know, is rather more prosaic.

To be sure, there are still a few mediaeval buildings in London but it is far from being the ancient capital that other cities in Europe still are. There is no mediaeval quarter, no walled enclave of narrow winding streets dominated by an historic citadel dating back hundreds of years. The Tower of London makes a very formidable citadel, and some of the streets around it are as narrow and winding as one could wish for, but the overall effect is certainly not mediaeval. Nor are there any ancient town houses in London, little changed in half a millenium, as there are in Florence or Venice; nor any mediaeval apartments that can still be rented, as in Rome. London isn't that kind of town.

Yet its origins are as ancient as any. It was founded by the Romans soon after 43 AD, as a commercial centre and sea port. The Romans chose a defensible position above the high-water mark, at a point where the river could still be bridged, and built a thriving town of some 330 acres, which was very large for the time. Roman London stretched from just beyond Fenchurch Street station in the east to St Paul's cathedral in the west. The original settlement was surrounded by a stone wall, inside which stood a fort, forum, basilica and governor's palace, as well as temples and public bath houses. Hardly any of it remains above ground

'IT WAS FOUNDED BY THE ROMANS SOON AFTER 43 AD, AS A COMMERCIAL CENTRE AND SEA PORT.'

NO EXPENSE WAS SPARED WHEN THE MIDLAND RAILWAY DECIDED TO BUILD A LONDON HOTEL AT ST PANCRAS STATION — THE GRAND MIDLAND HOTEL, WHICH OPENED IN 1873. THE HOTEL HAS BEEN CLOSED SINCE 1935, BUT THERE ARE PLANS TO REVIVE IT AS A TERMINAL HOTEL FOR THE CROSS-CHANNEL TRAIN LINK.

today, but property developers frequently discover Roman ruins six metres down, while digging the foundations for new office blocks.

After the Romans came the Danes, who razed London's walls to the ground in the 9th century; and King Alfred, who restored them again. After Alfred came Edward the Confessor, who began the construction of Westminster Abbey on a thorny island three miles west of the city. William the Conqueror arranged for himself to be crowned there before taking up temporary residence in the palace nearby, where the Houses of Parliament now stand. William also commissioned the building of the Tower of London, borrowing its revolutionary square design from the Byzantines, who had built similar fortresses in the Holy Land.

So London grew, piece by piece, always centred on the Tower and the old Roman walls, always clinging to the safety that the city's defences could provide. By the mid-1530s, when Henry VIII dissolved the monasteries, the area between Westminster and the City of London was still largely open space, a green belt of land between the ancient walls on one side and the growing nucleus of abbey buildings on the other. Inside the walls though, Londoners were packed to bursting point. The Great Plague of 1665 swept virtually unchecked through the narrow streets, killing 7000 people a week at its height, and was followed a year later by the Great Fire. The fire began in a bakery in Pudding Lane and continued at full spate for four days, destroying St Paul's cathedral, 89 other churches, and more than 13,000 private houses. By the time it had burned itself out, London, as a mediaeval city, had ceased to exist.

'WILLIAM ALSO COMMISSIONED THE BUILDING OF THE TOWER OF LONDON, BORROWING ITS REVOLUTIONARY SQUARE DESIGN FROM THE BYZANTINES, WHO HAD BUILT SIMILAR FORTRESSES IN THE HOLY LAND.'

Rebuilding began as soon as was practicable – rather too soon for some. In the rush to pick up the pieces, a great opportunity was missed to redesign the city along less haphazard lines. Sir Christopher Wren drew up a master plan, involving a unity of quays and avenues around St Paul's and the Royal Exchange. But his ideas expected too much from almost 100,000 homeless Londoners and were never carried out. Wren had to be content instead with rebuilding St Paul's, as well as 36 livery company halls and more than 50 parish churches. It was enough to keep him occupied for many years to come.

Much of his work still survives, mostly in the City, but also at Chelsea, where he was the principal architect for the Royal Hospital, a retirement home for old soldiers. It is from Wren's time onwards that London began to develop into the city still recognisable today. The 18th century saw a great deal of expansion, chiefly by aristocratic landowners who turned their open fields into housing estates at enormous profit to themselves. And the 19th saw the coming of the railways, with an explosion of red brick suburbs as Londoners began to commute long distances for the first time. The siting of the new railway termini was a problem though, for there was no way that railway lines could stretch into the heart of the city without severe disruption of existing architectural designs. One major consequence was an alliance of upper class landlords and middle class homeowners to ensure that the new railway stations were all built in working class areas, well away from themselves. As a result, London is very poorly served by railway stations in the centre. Not even the subsequent idea of putting the trains underground could do much to relieve the problem.

What remains then of historic London at the end of the 20th century? Plenty, in fact, if one is prepared to seek it out. To the obvious sights (Buckingham Palace, the Tower, Westminster Abbey, No 10 Downing Street) can be added a whole range of lesser buildings which somehow or other have escaped the urge to pull down and rebuild. The ruins of the Globe theatre have recently been discovered in Southwark, not far from the old coaching inn used by the Pickwick Club. Across the river, the tilt yard at Horse Guards parade is still there, where knightly tournaments were held in the Middle Ages and so too is the Admiralty building nearby, where Captain Cook and Lord Nelson received their orders.

'THE RUINS OF THE GLOBE THEATRE HAVE RECENTLY BEEN DISCOVERED IN SOUTHWARK, NOT FAR FROM THE OLD COACHING INN USED BY THE PICKWICK CLUB.'

Through Horse Guards arch, it is perfectly possible to stand where Samuel Pepys did to watch Charles I being executed outside the Banqueting House, or visit Westminster Hall further along, where Guy Fawkes and Sir Thomas More stood trial for their lives. Clive of India's house still stands in Berkeley Square, and Dr Johnson's near Fleet Street. Keats', Dickens', Gladstone's and the Duke of Wellington's houses are all still there; and so are Carlyle's and Karl Marx's.

The Old Curiosity Shop hasn't changed in centuries, and the warehouse where Jack the Ripper killed one of his victims still belongs to the same company. It is possible to walk exactly the same streets as the Ripper did, or follow in Boswell's footsteps on a night of amorous adventure, or trace the same route taken by Queen Anne in a sedan chair. Inevitably there is the roar of traffic in the background, and hurtling lorries to avoid, and glass and concrete where once was mellow brick. But historic London is still there, where it has always been, for those who care to go out and look for it.

TOWER OF LONDON

t looks relatively insignificant from the air, but for hundreds of years the Tower dominated the City of London as no other building has ever done. The central White Tower was built by William the Conqueror on the site of a Roman bastion and the surrounding fortifications were greatly enlarged by his successors. The Tower has been zoo, palace, treasury and prison in its time, sometimes all of these together. Henry VI was murdered there, as were the two little Princes. Anne Boleyn, Catherine Howard and Lady Jane Grey were beheaded on the green, Sir Thomas More on Tower Hill outside. Most prisoners were taken to the Tower by water, entering through the infamous Traitors' Gate. The place is a museum now, although the Crown Jewels are still kept there under military guard, as they have been since 1303.

St Paul's Cathedral

educed to a heap of rubble by the Great Fire of 1666, St Paul's soon rose again under the direction of Sir Christopher Wren. The foundation stone was laid in 1675 and the topping out ceremony was completed by Wren's son in 1708. Wren was forced to accept all sorts of compromises to his original design, but the result – even though it wasn't exactly as he wanted – is undoubtedly a masterpiece. Particularly noticeable from the air is the false outer wall, concealing the buttresses behind. Wren himself is buried in the crypt of the cathedral, as are Lord Nelson, the Duke of Wellington and other national figures. The central dome became a symbol of defiance during the 1940 Blitz, surviving unscathed while buildings all around lay in ruins.

(LEFT) 'SI MONUMENTUM REQUIRIS, CIRCUMSPICE,' ARE THE WORDS ON WREN'S TOMB IN THE CRYPT. IF YOU SEEK MY MONUMENT, LOOK AROUND.

(FAR LEFT) PRISONERS HAVE BEEN KEPT IN THE TOWER AS LATE AS THE 20TH CENTURY, INCLUDING RUDOLF HESS IN 1941.

ROYAL HOSPITAL, CHELSEA

 harles II commissioned the Royal Hospital at Chelsea as a retirement home for old soldiers. The idea was inspired by Louis XIV's Invalides and was later copied at the Royal Naval Hospital, Greenwich. Several architects worked on the project, but the chief of them was Sir Christopher Wren. Some 200 old soldiers, known as Chelsea Pensioners, live at the Hospital and they are famous for the scarlet coats and tricorn hats worn on ceremonial occasions. All the major battles in which the Pensioners took part, from 1662 to the Korean War, are commemorated on the walls, and the names of the Pensioners who fought are listed. Until recently, the oldest pensioner was a veteran of the Boer War.

(BELOW) THE ADMIRALTY BUILDING, LEFT OF THE OLD TILT YARD, IS WHERE CAPTAIN COOK AND LORD NELSON CAME TO RECEIVE THEIR ORDERS.

(RIGHT) THE RANELAGH GARDENS, VERY POPULAR IN THE 18TH CENTURY, FLOURISHED IN THE GROUNDS OF THE ROYAL HOSPITAL.

ST JAMES'S PARK

 t James's Park is a blessing to Londoners, an open public space with Buckingham Palace at one end and Whitehall and Downing Street at the other. It was a marsh until Henry VIII drained it for a private deer park. James I kept camels there, and crocodiles in the lake. Charles I walked through the park from St James's Palace to Whitehall on the morning of his execution (the Banqueting House where he died is visible behind the Horse Guards building on the right of the picture). His son Charles II opened the park to the public and it has remained open ever since. The open space on the right is a former tilt yard, used for jousting in mediaeval times. The Queen's Birthday Parade (Trooping the Colour) is held there every June.

No. 10
DOWNING STREET

verlooking St James's Park, with the bulk of the Foreign Office on its left, and the mediaeval tilt yard on its right, Downing Street seems comparatively insignificant from the air. But it contains in No 10 the most famous private address in the country. British Prime Ministers have lived there ever since 1735. The house is modest by the standards of many Governments – deliberately so, since the Prime Minister is only a public servant. It is for the Queen, as Head of State, to live grandly. Nevertheless, No 10 is larger than it appears at first glance, with a warren of offices behind and secret passages that can be used in emergency. The Chancellor of the Exchequer lives next door at No 11, and the old Treasury building fronts the main road along Whitehall.

DOWNING STREET IS NAMED FOR A HARVARD MAN, GEORGE DOWNING. AFTER FAILING IN THE COLONIES, HE RETURNED TO ENGLAND IN THE 1640S AND BECAME A PROPERTY DEVELOPER, AMONG OTHER THINGS.

CHAPTER FOUR

EAST ANGLIA
THE NATION'S GRANARY

'ery flat,' was Noel Coward's verdict on East Anglia, Norfolk in particular, and flat it certainly is – so flat that the east wind blowing across the fens comes directly from Siberia, with nothing to stop it in between. So flat also that sea walls have had to be built, Dutch-style, to prevent the North Sea flooding across the plains. It was the Dutch who did the work, since they had the expertise, and their influence in this part of England has always been strong, both in the architecture of towns such as King's Lynn, and in the stolid blond faces and undemonstrative natures of the people who live there.

Undemonstrative, but in no way downtrodden. The people of East Anglia have always been as quietly determined as any in Britain. When William the Conqueror came to the island stronghold of Ely, surrounded then by unpredictable swamps, he found it one of the last centres of opposition to Norman rule, stoutly defended by Hereward the Wake and a small group of followers. William succeeded in bridging the swamps, and Ely fell, but Hereward escaped and has been a folk hero ever since. It was said of Hereward that another three like him and England would never have been conquered, although contemporary evidence suggests that he was little more than a local brigand, much more interested in plunder than principle.

'IT WAS THE DUTCH WHO DID THE WORK, SINCE THEY HAD THE EXPERTISE, AND THEIR INFLUENCE IN THIS PART OF ENGLAND HAS ALWAYS BEEN STRONG...'

William's base for the siege of Ely was Cambridge, a Celtic settlement on the river Cam, later developed by the Romans as the last viable trading point before the fens to the north. Immediately south of the town stood a large forest, which subsequent generations found useful against Viking attack. By the time a group of dissident Oxford scholars settled there in 1209, Cambridge was already a thriving market town. Once the university was established, it never looked back.

Many of the university's present buildings date only from the 18th or 19th centuries, but a handful of much older ones still remain. The most famous is King's College Chapel, begun by Henry VI in 1446 (he laid the foundation stone in person) and completed several monarchs later in 1536. The stonework changes

THE ELY CATHEDRAL WAS FIRST BEGUN BY ST ETHELDREDA IN 673. THE CENTRAL TOWER COLLAPSED IN 1322 AND WAS REPLACED BY THE OCTAGONAL LANTERN, WHICH IS NOW THE CATHEDRAL'S MOST SPECTACULAR FEATURE.

colour halfway up the walls, indicating a lengthy gap during the Wars of the Roses when finances ran out and the work was abandoned until it was safe to proceed again, with a different supply of stone. Other original buildings remain also, notably the 14th century Old Court at Corpus Christi college, where Christopher Marlowe's rooms can still be seen, and the 16th century Great Court at Trinity, where Sir Isaac Newton's rooms remain pretty much as he left them.

Beyond Cambridge, East Anglia opens onto a vast prairie land that stretches almost uninterrupted towards Yarmouth and the North Sea. The forest south of Cambridge has long gone – the view from the Old Vicarage, Grantchester, where Rupert Brooke once had a room, is now of open fields towards the spires of King's College Chapel – and so have other forests as well. When Elizabeth I made her progress into Suffolk 400 years ago, it was noted that her travels took her through almost continuous woodland. The same route today would reveal scarcely a tree standing in any direction.

'BY THE TIME A GROUP OF DISSIDENT OXFORD SCHOLARS SETTLED THERE IN 1209, CAMBRIDGE WAS ALREADY A THRIVING MARKET TOWN.'

The forests were cut down for fuel and housing and were not replaced. Instead they were planted with acres of wheat and barley, which grows very efficiently on the clay of Norfolk and Suffolk. Eighteenth century landlords such as 'Turnip' Townshend and Coke of Holkham spent much time and energy experimenting with different types of crop rotation on their estates, with results that are still in use today. They built fine houses for themselves as well – Holkham, Ickworth, Houghton Hall (home of Sir Robert Walpole) – often incorporating Italian ideas of design picked up during their grand tours abroad.

But it is to another agricultural product that East Anglia owes much of its special character: wool. Not, on the face of it, a very interesting product, yet the source of considerable prosperity to East Anglians from the Middle Ages onwards. So important was wool to the national economy in fact that to this day the Lord Chancellor sits on the Woolsack in the House of Lords, a visual reminder to Parliament of where the people's interests lie. For centuries East Anglia was a centre of the cloth trade, exporting to every country in Europe, growing sleek and comfortable on the proceeds. Saffron Walden in Essex even owes its name to the local crop used in the dyeing process. It owes many of its fine buildings as well, as do towns such as Thaxted in Essex and Lavenham and Long Melford in Suffolk.

For an idea of what East Anglia looked like in those prosperous times, one only has to see the paintings of John Constable and Thomas Gainsborough (himself the son of a wool manufacturer), both of whom were born and bred in

Suffolk and did much of their best work there. Constable devoted his life to landscape painting, although he never achieved much success in his own time. In 1821 he exhibited a picture of his father's watermill at Flatford (still there today). The picture was entitled *A Landscape – Noon*, and was considered so unremarkable that only a Frenchman could be persuaded to buy it. Today it is called *The Hay Wain* and is a national treasure.

Gainsborough too was a keen landscape painter, although circumstances forced him to earn his living as a portraitist. Perhaps his most distinguished work is of an old schoolfriend and his wife, *Mr and Mrs Andrews*, painted on their estate outside Sudbury. The portrait is justly famous, but it is the land in the background that Gainsborough knew and loved.

Others loved it too, for East Anglia has always been a magnet for artists of all kinds, whether painters, sculptors or simple architects in stone. The quality of light is said to be better than in other parts of England and the beauty of the landscape is beyond dispute. The architects of Ely Cathedral, which dates from the 11th century onwards, were plainly engaged on a work of art, as the results testify. So too were the architects of Norwich, whose cathedral spire rises some 315 feet above the town. The Close at Norwich – where Lord Nelson received his early education – must rank as one of the half dozen most beautiful in the country, on a par with Winchester, York and Canterbury.

'THE QUALITY OF LIGHT IS SAID TO BE BETTER THAN IN OTHER PARTS OF ENGLAND AND THE BEAUTY OF THE LANDSCAPE IS BEYOND DISPUTE.'

On a less elevated plane, but almost as intriguing, is the model holiday village of Thorpeness, on the Suffolk coast. Thorpeness was designed before the First World War as a single entity – a collection of mock-Tudor holiday homes with a strong German influence, set around a 65 acre artificial lake. The result is surprisingly attractive, even though the war prevented completion of later phases.

The oddest building of all at Thorpeness, and certainly the most engaging, is the 'house in the clouds' (an old water tower disguised as a house from a fairy tale), which stands across the lane from a still-operative 19th century windmill. Together with the ancient moot hall at Aldeburgh, a couple of miles along the coast, and the maltings at Snape, they sum up a style of architecture both agreeably eccentric and uniquely East Anglian. It is interesting to note though that the moot hall, which once stood in the centre of Aldeburgh, is now only a few yards from the sea. Another 400 years, at the present rate of erosion, and it will almost certainly be lost underwater.

CAMBRIDGE

here has been a settlement at Cambridge since before the Romans, but it wasn't until 1209, when a group of dissident scholars arrived from Oxford to set up a new university, that the town began to expand. The oldest surviving university building is a house in the grounds of St John's College, the 'School of Pythagoras', which dates from the 12th century. Several college courts are almost as old, and the rooms used by Christopher Marlowe and Sir Isaac Newton are still in use today. King's College Chapel, pictured here, was begun by Henry VI in 1446. Work was frequently suspended during the Wars of the Roses, so the building was not finally completed until 1536. Cambridge's punts, ideal for poling through the shallow waters of the Fens, are now used mainly by tourists.

'THE OLDEST SURVIVING UNIVERSITY BUILDING IS A HOUSE IN THE GROUNDS OF ST JOHN'S COLLEGE, THE 'SCHOOL OF PYTHAGORAS', WHICH DATES FROM THE 12TH CENTURY.'

THE ART OF THE ITALIAN RENAISSANCE FLOURISHED AGAINST A BACKDROP OF POLITICAL AND ECONOMIC ANARCHY. SO TOO IN CAMBRIDGE, KING'S COLLEGE CHAPEL GREW OUT OF THE WARS OF THE ROSES.

ICKWORTH

ckworth was never meant to be a country house. It was designed much more as a showcase for some spectacular works of art. The land had been in the Earl of Bristol's family since the 15th century, but it was not until 1795 that the 4th Earl commissioned the rotunda and flanking galleries to accommodate the paintings and sculptures he was amassing in Italy. The Earl was an eccentric figure who had taken holy orders and risen to become Bishop of Derry, but chose to make his home in Italy. There he enjoyed the food and wine so much that Hotels Bristol sprang up all over Europe as a sign of good living. Sadly, he also died in Italy, having survived just long enough to see his beloved Titians and Raphaels seized by the French army. The collection was dispersed and never reached its intended home.

THE HOUSE IS 200 YARDS LONG AND THE CENTRAL DOME MORE THAN 100 FEET HIGH. IT LOOKS VERY GRAND, BUT IS NOT PARTICULARLY COMFORTABLE TO LIVE IN.

SAFFRON WALDEN

ven from the air, Saffron Walden's church spire makes a splendid landmark, standing almost 200 feet above the rest of the town. It was added in 1831 to the mediaeval church, where Henry VIII's chancellor Lord Audley is buried. The town takes its name from the saffron crocus, imported by the Crusaders for use as a dye in the woollen industry. It enjoyed considerable prosperity in the Middle Ages, as numerous buildings still testify. Indeed the combination of mediaeval half-timbering and Georgian brick makes Saffron Walden one of the prettiest market towns in the country. Oliver Cromwell's reputed headquarters, the Sun Inn, stands much as it did, famous for its ornamental pargeting. Near the ruins of the castle there is an old 'maze' in the chalk, constructed hundreds of years ago for no known purpose that anyone can discern.

THE CHURCH WAS REBUILT BETWEEN 1450 AND 1550 IN THE PERPINDICULAR STYLE.

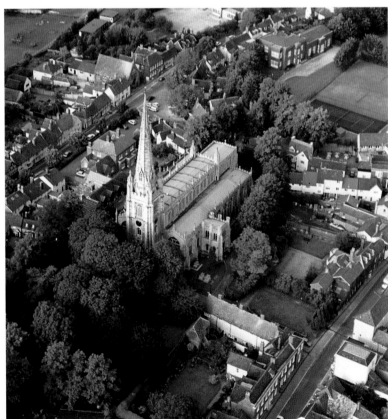

CHAPTER FIVE

THE WEST MIDLANDS

SHAKESPEARE COUNTRY

nglish kings have suffered a variety of dreadful fates over the years. They have been strangled, beheaded, shot in the eye, starved to death, suffocated while asleep, hacked to pieces in battle. They have died in all sorts of ghoulish and unpleasant ways. But none of them ever died as horribly as Edward II. On 21 September 1327, in the heart of the Gloucestershire countryside, he was seized from his bed in Berkeley Castle and forcibly held down while a red hot spitting iron was shoved into his anus.

Edward was not a good king. He was weak and foolish, idle and dissolute. He was congenitally incapable of giving a lead to his people, preferring instead to spend his time with his boyfriends, of whom Piers Gaveston was his especial favourite. After Gaveston was executed by political rivals, he transferred his attentions to a young man named Hugh Despenser, with equally unfortunate results. His one attempt at leadership, in a very undistinguished reign, was to wage war against the Scots – a disastrous venture which resulted in the annihilation of the English army at Bannockburn and guaranteed the survival of an independent Scotland for another 400 years.

Inevitably Edward made enemies. Chief among them was his own wife, Isabella, who plotted with her lover Mortimer to depose Edward and install her son on the throne instead. At Isabella's behest, Edward was seized and taken to Berkeley, where his gaolers kept him half-starved and deprived of sleep and clothing. They locked him in a filthy room over a charnel house, in the hope that he would die of plague. When that failed, they decided to kill him instead with a spitting iron, so as to leave no suspicious marks on the body. He shrieked so loudly when they held him down that his screams were clearly audible outside the castle. There are people living nearby who claim they can hear them to this day.

'THIS PART OF ENGLAND HAS ALWAYS SEEMED ESPECIALLY SUITED TO GRAND COUNTRY HOUSES, PERHAPS BECAUSE OF THE ROLLING LANDSCAPE AND THE ATTRACTIVENESS OF LOCAL BUILDING MATERIALS.'

ONCE A SLEEPY MARKET TOWN, STRATFORD-ON-AVON IS NOW A MAJOR TOURIST DESTINATION AND HOUSE TO THE ROYAL SHAKESPEARE COMPANY'S THEATRE ON THE BANKS OF THE RIVER.

Yet looking at the castle now, still inhabited by the Berkeley family, it is hard to believe that it was ever the setting for such appalling brutality. Gloucestershire is one of the prettiest counties of middle England, and the town of Berkeley is as tranquil as any. Many of the town's buildings are Georgian in origin, and the ancient church still retains some of its Norman features. The inventor of vaccination, Edward Jenner, is buried there, near the chancel.

So pretty is the surrounding countryside in fact that several of the modern royal family keep country homes there, secure in the knowledge that whatever else may happen, they are unlikely to be assaulted with a spitting iron. This part of England has always seemed especially suited to grand country houses, perhaps because of the rolling landscape and the attractiveness of local building materials. Badminton House is one of the best known examples. It was built for the 1st Duke of Beaufort in 1682 and is approached by a spectacular three mile avenue of beech trees. Hidcote too, with its splendid gardens, is very striking. And the onion domes of Sezincote – financed 200 years ago with loot brought back from India – blend especially well with the Indian-style garden laid out by Humphrey Repton.

'TO THE NORTH ALSO, THE COUNTIES OF HEREFORD AND WORCESTER ARE AS PRETTY AS ANY IN ENGLAND, WITH A CHOCOLATE BOX LANDSCAPE AND BUILDINGS TO MATCH.'

To the north also, the counties of Hereford and Worcester are as pretty as any in England, with a chocolate box landscape and buildings to match. For a near-perfect example of a 14th century house, the black and white timber framed manor at Lower Brockhampton is hard to beat. A few miles away, the architecture of Madresfield Court, equally eclectic, reflects the fluctuating fortunes of the Lygon family (Earls Beauchamp), who have lived there since 1260. Evelyn Waugh stayed at Madresfield as a young man, with his friend Hugh Lygon. He was so impressed, both by the family and the house, that he sat down years later and wrote about them all in *Brideshead Revisited*.

Madresfield is in Worcestershire, within sight of the Malvern Hills, where Sir Edward Elgar found the inspiration for some of his greatest music. William Langland too is said to have composed much of his late 14th century poem *Piers Plowman* while enjoying the view from the Worcestershire Beacon. On a clear day, he might have seen as far across the Vale of Evesham as Compton Wynyates, one of the most visually satisfying of all England's stately homes. The house stands in Warwickshire, with an ancient church in the background and a windmill on the crest behind. It was rebuilt in the 15th century, but the property has belonged to the Marquess of Northampton's family since at least 1204. Cromwellian troops used it as a barracks during the Civil War. They only returned it to the rightful owner on condition that the moat was filled in and a huge fine paid.

But it is for Stratford-upon-Avon that Warwickshire is best known, the town where William Shakespeare was born and grew up. He is said to have been born in a house, still standing, in Henley Street, although there is no evidence that the family owned it before William was 11 years old. But he was certainly baptised in the town church, and buried there too. Anne Hathaway's cottage, which belonged to his father-in-law, can still be seen, and so can Hall's Croft, a large gabled house which belonged to Shakespeare's son-in-law. The Bard himself, after making his fortune in London, retired to New Place, the grandest house in the town, which unfortunately was demolished in the 18th century.

'BUT IT IS FOR STRATFORD-UPON-AVON THAT WARWICKSHIRE IS BEST KNOWN, THE TOWN WHERE WILLIAM SHAKESPEARE WAS BORN AND GREW UP.'

Just outside Stratford though, Charlecote Hall still remains, home of the Lucy family for 700 years. The young Shakespeare is said to have poached deer from the estate (an offence punishable then as now by a hefty fine and several months' imprisonment). It is thought that he originally left for London not so much to seek his fortune as to escape the wrath of Sir Thomas Lucy, who wanted him flogged for his crimes.

Whatever the facts, it is certainly true that the unkind portrait of Justice Shallow in *Henry IV Part 2* and *The Merry Wives of Windsor* is a devastatingly accurate image of Sir Thomas. The 'three luces hauriant argent' on the Lucy coat of arms even became 'three louses rampant' in the plays. Shakespeare always liked to settle old scores in his work. He enjoyed making dramas out of history too. One wonders what he would have made of the happenings at Berkeley Castle if he had only had the chance. He never did though, because his exact contemporary, Christopher Marlowe, beat him to it with *The Troublesome Raigne and Lamentable Death of Edward the Second*.

BERKELEY CASTLE

et in the heart of the Gloucestershire countryside, Berkeley was the scene of the infamous murder of Edward II in 1327, when the King was forcibly skewered with a red hot spitting iron. Unfortunately, the exact site of the crime has been altered since Edward's time, because the castle was gutted a few years later and rebuilt within the same walls. The King died in a tiny cell, today incorporated into a larger room known as 'the King's gallery'. Thomas, Lord Berkeley, claimed he was not in residence at the time and knew nothing of the murder. But a study of the household records indicates not only that he was there, but that he also sent one of the murderers to Nottingham to deliver the news of the King's death in person to the Queen and her lover, Mortimer.

THE CASTLE WAS EXPENSIVELY ALTERED AFTER EDWARD II'S MURDER — A REWARD PERHAPS FOR THE BERKELEY FAMILY KEEPING QUIET ABOUT WHAT HAD HAPPENED.

CHELTENHAM

enteel and cultured, the spa of Cheltenham has long endured a reputation as a retirement home for the middle classes, a place where colonels from the Indian Army go to die. This is not entirely fanciful, for many of them had liver complaints from the tropics and the waters of Cheltenham Spa are highly beneficial. The mineral content was first noticed in 1716, reputedly by observing the drinking habits of some healthy-looking pigeons. A pump room opened in 1738 and the original Cotswold village was largely rebuilt in the early 19th century, transformed into an elegant Regency town of taste and refinement. For many people though, the most interesting thing about Cheltenham is its splendid racecourse at Prestbury Park. The Cheltenham Gold Cup is held there every year, one of the main events of the jumping season. By long tradition it is always attended by hordes of Irish, who come over by the boatload and have the time of their lives before going back home again.

THE CHELTENHAM GOLD CUP IS A MUST IN EVERY RACEGOER'S CALENDAR. THE QUEEN MOTHER ATTENDS EVERY YEAR, AS DO OTHER MEMBERS OF THE ROYAL FAMILY.

CLIFTON SUSPENSION
BRIDGE

panning the Avon gorge between Gloucestershire and Somerset, Clifton was one of the wonders of the world when it was built – the largest single-span bridge ever attempted. It was the brainchild of Isambard Kingdom Brunel, who was only 23 when he had the idea. His first design was rejected, but he submitted a second in 1831, which was accepted as being the most mathematically sound of all the designs considered (sounder even than one by Thomas Telford). Work began in 1836, but soon stopped again for lack of money. Not until 1864 was the bridge finally completed, using materials taken from the Hungerford suspension bridge in London. Sadly, Brunel was already dead by then, having never set eyes on one of his most enduring creations.

THE BRIDGE IS NOT FOR THE FAINT-HEARTED. IT STANDS 245 FEET ABOVE THE GORGE, WHICH MAKES IT A FAVOURITE WITH BUNGEE JUMPERS.

MADRESFIELD COURT

adresfield (the name means 'field of the mowers') dates from Tudor times, but was greatly extended in the Victorian era. It was the home for centuries of the Lygon family (Earls Beauchamp). Hugh Lygon was a close friend of Evelyn Waugh's, who often came to stay after the breakdown of his first marriage. The family remember him working on *Black Mischief* while he was

there: 'He wrote slowly and reluctantly... groaning loudly as he shut himself away in what had been the day nursery for a few hours every day'. The household was somewhat eccentric in Waugh's time, Lord Beauchamp having retired to Italy to avoid a homosexual scandal, Lady Beauchamp living elsewhere with her brother. Waugh was so intrigued that he borrowed the whole story and used it much later in *Brideshead Revisited*.

'IT IS ONLY FIVE WEEKS SINCE I LEFT MADRESFIELD,' WROTE WAUGH IN BRITISH GUIANA. 'INSTEAD OF THE SMILING MEADOWS OF WORCESTERSHIRE AND THE NOBLE LINE OF THE MALVERN HILLS THAT I LOVE SO DEARLY, I LOOK OUT UPON A LIMITLESS SWAMP.'

SEZINCOTE

aking its name from the 'hillside of the oaks', Sezincote is the work of the Cockerell brothers, Samuel and Charles, great-great nephews of Samuel Pepys. Samuel Cockerell was an architect, numbering Warren Hastings among his clients. Charles was a nabob (later a baronet and Member of Parliament), newly returned from making his fortune with the East India Company. Together they set out to remodel the existing house at Sezincote into something far more exotic, employing the Indian themes fashionable at the time. Work began in 1805 and the Prince Regent was a guest at the house soon afterwards, probably in 1806. He was so impressed by the onion dome that he later commissioned John Nash to redesign the exterior of the Brighton Pavilion in similar, though more lavish style.

'A GOOD JOKE, BUT A GOOD HOUSE TOO'. UNUSUALLY FOR A COUNTRY ESTATE, THE MAIN HOUSE FACES EAST INSTEAD OF SOUTH.

WARWICK CASTLE

ew castles can be more glamorous or better preserved than Warwick, built on a majestic site overlooking the river Avon. First defended by the Saxons against Viking invaders, the place has been a fortress ever since and still retains architecture from every period of its development. The mediaeval lavatories still work and the dungeons could easily be used for their original purpose. Richard Neville (Warwick, the Kingmaker) was lord of the castle until his death in the Wars of the Roses. The 2nd Lord Brooke held it for Parliament during the Civil War, until he too was killed at the battle of Lichfield. In happier times, Daisy, Countess of Warwick, is remembered for the dazzling parties she gave at the castle, often herself ending up in bed with her lover, the future Edward VII.

RICHARD III IS SAID TO HAVE BUILT A GARDEN AT THE FOOT OF THE MOUND (COVERED IN TREES AT THE LEFT) FOR HIS WIFE, DAUGHTER OF WARWICK THE KINGMAKER.

STRATFORD-ON-AVON

O n the banks of the Avon stands Holy Trinity Church, where the infant William Shakespeare was baptised in 1564 and where, in 1616, he was buried. Shakespeare probably left Stratford in his late teens, but had made enough money by 1597 to return and buy New Place, the town's finest house. His tomb in the church bears these words:

Good frend for Jesus sake forebeare
To digg the dust encloased heare!
Bleste be the man that spares the stones
And curst be he that moves my bones.

HOLY TRINITY CHURCH DATES FROM THE 13TH CENTURY. ITS SIZE INDICATES THAT STRATFORD WAS A PROSPEROUS TOWN, EVEN THEN.

CHAPTER SIX

NORTH FROM THE THAMES VALLEY

THE HEART OF ENGLAND

he name Despenser has featured twice in British history, neither time with any great distinction. Hugh Despenser, as already noted, was a close confidant of Edward II and came to a bad end when both he and his father were seized by the king's enemies and hanged. For the next 400 years, nothing more was heard of the name in public life. Then another Despenser emerged, with results equally unedifying, if also rather intriguing. This was the eighth Baron LeDespencer (sic), better known to posterity as Sir Francis Dashwood, founder and moving spirit of the Hellfire Club.

Dashwood was born in 1708 and succeeded to his father's baronetcy in 1724. He also succeeded to a vast fortune, which enabled him to do exactly as he wished all his life, with never any heed for the consequences. On a grand tour of Europe as a young man, he was so amused at the sight of penitents in the Sistine chapel, begging punishment for their sins, that he laid into them with a horsewhip, since that was clearly what they wanted. The Vatican authorities promptly deported him from Rome, with instructions never to set foot in Italy again. Dashwood went quietly, but took with him a love-hate relationship with the Catholic church that was to last all his life.

> 'FOR THE NEXT 400 YEARS, NOTHING MORE WAS HEARD OF THE NAME IN PUBLIC LIFE. THEN ANOTHER DESPENSER EMERGED, WITH RESULTS EQUALLY UNEDIFYING, IF ALSO RATHER INTRIGUING.'

Back in England, he established the Hellfire Club for his aristocratic friends. It was a quasi-religious order, dedicated to Satanism and Black Magic, but with a great deal of drinking and whoring thrown in. Members dressed as monks and amused themselves by deflowering virgins on the altar at midnight. At first they held their meetings at Medmenham, a ruined Norman abbey on the banks of the Thames. But their doings became so notorious – particularly when members of the Government were involved – that crowds of sightseers turned out to watch, which inevitably put a damper on proceedings. So Sir Francis looked around for

ACROSS THE RIVER FROM WINDSOR LIES ETON COLLEGE. IT WAS FOUNDED IN 1440 BY HENRY VI, WHO COMMISSIONED THE CHAPEL IN THE CENTRE OF THE PICTURE (VERY LIKE HIS OTHER FOUNDATION, KING'S COLLEGE CHAPEL, IN CAMBRIDGE).

another, more private venue, and found one on his estate at West Wycombe in Buckinghamshire.

In a chalk hill on the estate, deep below the surface of the earth, he hollowed out an elaborate series of caves and chambers in the shape of a woman's reproductive system. Here, 200 feet beneath the Dashwood family church on top of the hill, the members of the Hellfire Club wore blood-red robes and advanced by candlelight to the 'Inner Temple', where they celebrated Black Mass and made sacrifices to the god of virginity before getting to grips with the young women they had brought with them. If there were no village girls available, they imported 'nuns' from London – prostitutes, many of whom were adept at faking loss of innocence.

And who were these people, who behaved so vilely? Well, the Earl of Bute was Prime Minister, and Dashwood was Chancellor of the Exchequer. The Earl of Sandwich was First Lord of the Admiralty, and John Wilkes was a noted Parliamentarian and champion of liberty. Benjamin Franklin was a frequent guest of Sir Francis, although the evidence is inconclusive as to whether or not he participated in orgies. He certainly visited the caves and knew all about them. It was at Wycombe, somewhat incongruously, that he and Sir Francis had the idea for the *Franklin Prayer Book*, which became the basis for the *Book of Common Prayer* used by most American Protestants ever since.

Today the caves can still be seen at West Wycombe, as can the house and the church, with its golden globe 20 feet in diameter, where club members sometimes locked themselves in with a supply of booze and women. The gardens are still there too, although no longer laid out in the shape of a naked girl, as they were in Sir Francis's time. Gone too is the garden temple with an entrance like a woman's, and the phallic column in front of it. In fact little remains except the caves, which are very much as Sir Francis left them. They provide a steady source of income for the Dashwood family, who continue to live at West Wycombe Park, albeit rather less flamboyantly than their ancestors.

It might be thought that such goings on among members of the Government were strictly an 18th century phenomenon, a reflection of the licentious times they lived in but this is not so. An easy walk from West Wycombe is Bradenham Manor, where the young Benjamin Disraeli enjoyed plenty of feminine company at his father's house before his marriage in 1839. And a few miles down the road lies Cliveden, near Taplow, the scene of an extraordinary sexual scandal which rocked the British establishment in the 1960s and led within months to the downfall of the Conservative government.

Now a hotel, Cliveden was then a stately home belonging to the 3rd Viscount Astor, himself a Member of Parliament before his elevation to the House of Lords. It was there, in the summer of 1961, that a beautiful young girl named Christine Keeler was frolicking naked in the swimming pool when she was surprised by Lord Astor and his guests, one of whom was the Minister for War, John Profumo. The attraction was instant, if one-sided. Profumo soon became Keeler's lover, a privilege he shared with several others, including the naval attache at the Russian embassy. When the newspapers got hold of the story, Profumo made a statement to the House of Commons denying that he had ever had anything to do with the girl. He was unmasked and forced to resign. The ensuing furore – avidly followed by President Kennedy, among others – cost the Government the next election and brought 13 years of Conservative rule to an end.

Scandals apart though, Buckinghamshire is a rather dull county, over-populated and with little scenery to recommend it. The most it can boast is Stowe school, once the home of the Dukes of Buckingham, and Chequers, the Prime Minister's official country residence, a 15th century manor house presented to the nation in thanksgiving for the end of the First World War. Lady Mary Grey, sister of the ill-fated Jane, was kept there in disgrace after making a secret marriage of which Queen Elizabeth I did not approve.

'THE ENSUING FURORE – AVIDLY FOLLOWED BY PRESIDENT KENNEDY, AMONG OTHERS – COST THE GOVERNMENT THE NEXT ELECTION AND BROUGHT 13 YEARS OF CONSERVATIVE RULE TO AN END.'

Elizabeth herself spent much of her own youth not far away, as a virtual prisoner at the Old Palace at Hatfield, in Hertfordshire. It was at Hatfield Park that she heard the news of her accession to the throne. The remains of the oak tree where she was sitting are carefully preserved near Hatfield House, which was built by one of her ministers, Robert Cecil, 1st Earl of Salisbury, at the turn of the 17th century. His father, William Cecil, built Burghley House in Northamptonshire. Both are splendid examples of Elizabethan architecture on a grand scale, and both still belong to different branches of the Cecil family.

The oak tree incidentally used to have a parallel in Kenya, where a plaque commemorated the fig tree at Treetops where the second Queen Elizabeth was staying when she succeeded to the throne. Unfortunately nothing remains of it now, because the tree was knocked down by a marauding elephant and a new Treetops was built the other side of the clearing.

HENLEY

enley is a pretty little town in the Thames Valley, famed for a stretch of river that continues upstream for more than a mile without a bend. Oxford and Cambridge held their first boat race there in 1829. Ten years later, the townspeople decided to stage a regatta every summer for the encouragement of trade. Today the regatta is a major event in the English social calendar. Oarsmen compete from all over the world, drawn by the combination of style and eccentricity (it is traditional for male spectators to dress in the clothes of the 1930s) that makes it a unique occasion. The competitors' boats for the regatta are accommodated in huge blue and white striped tents, pitched just above Henley's 18th century bridge.

THE BRIDGE IS DECORATED WITH MASKS OF FATHER THAMES AND THE GODDESS ISIS. THEY WERE THE WORK OF THE SCULPTRESS ANNE DAMER, A FRIEND OF NELSON AND NAPOLEON.

CLIVEDEN

 liveden was built for the
Duke of Sunderland in the
1850s, in the style of an
Italian Renaissance palace. It
was sold later to William Waldorf Astor,
formerly US ambassador to Italy, who took
British citizenship in 1899 and bought
himself a peerage during the Great War.
The house was known for the Cliveden set,
a gathering of politicians and statesmen
who weekended there in the 1920s. But its
main claim to fame lies in the swimming
pool, where a beautiful young girl,
Christine Keeler, was frolicking naked in
1961 when she caught the eye of the then
Minister for War, John Profumo. The
ensuing scandal led to the suicide of
Stephen Ward, Keeler's protector, and soon
afterwards to the fall of the Government.

'THE HOUSE WAS KNOWN
FOR THE CLIVEDEN SET, A
GATHERING OF POLITICIANS
AND STATESMEN WHO
WEEKENDED THERE IN THE
1920S.'

THE TUNE 'RULE
BRITANNIA' WAS FIRST
PERFORMED IN THE GROUNDS
HERE IN 1740. GLADSTONE
LIKED THE HOUSE SO MUCH
THAT HE WROTE A MESSAGE
OF APPROVAL ON THE WALL
— IN LATIN.

MENTMORE TOWERS

entmore looks very grand, very ancient, but dates only from the 1850s, when Meyer de Rothschild decided to build a country house for his family, within easy reach of London. The land was bought by his mother, a keen countrywoman, who thought her son should do some hunting at weekends, to take his mind off his banking affairs in the City. So Mentmore was designed initially as a hunting lodge, albeit on a lavish scale. With the Rothschild fortune behind him, Meyer hired Sir Joseph Paxton as architect and told him money was no object. The result was probably the finest neo-Jacobean building in the country – closely based on Wollaton Hall in Nottinghamshire – with staircases of Sicilian marble, panels of Genoese velvet, and a splendid fireplace imported from Rubens' house in Antwerp.

MENTMORE LATER BELONGED TO THE PRIME MINISTER LORD ROSEBERY, WHO HAD MARRIED INTO THE ROTHSCHILDS. NAPOLEON III, CZAR NICHOLAS II AND WINSTON CHURCHILL WERE ALL WEEKEND GUESTS THERE.

STRATFIELD SAYE

 tratfield Saye was a gift to the Duke of Wellington from a grateful nation, a country estate voted by Parliament for the victor of Waterloo. The original plan had been to build him a much larger house, along the lines of Blenheim Palace (built to commemorate the Duke of Marlborough's great victories). But it proved impossible to find a grand enough site not overshadowed by other houses nearby, so the existing Stratfield estate was bought instead. The Duke thought it rather poky, as did Queen Victoria and Sir Robert Peel. Copenhagen, Wellington's horse at Waterloo, is buried in the Ice House paddock, his grave marked by a turkey oak. The main house still contains many of Wellington's possessions (and some of Napoleon's) as well as two radiators installed by the Duke, which still work.

'VERY IMPOSING,' WAS THE AGENT'S DESCRIPTION, WHEN WELLINGTON BOUGHT STRATFIELD SAYE. 'A PRINCELY POSSESSION, AND VERY MUCH SUPERIOR TO ANY OTHER PROPERTY.'

WEST WYCOMBE PARK

 n a hill above the Hell Fire caves stands St Lawrence's, the church that belongs to the Dashwood family. Members of the Hell Fire club – among them an 18th century Prime Minister and a Chancellor of the Exchequer – are said to have locked themselves in the church tower with a plentiful supply of drink and women. The church is clearly visible from West Wycombe park, home of the club's founder, Sir Francis Dashwood. He once took a clergyman to the top of a phallic-looking tower to show him the gardens laid out in the shape of a naked woman. It was in this unlikely setting that Sir Francis and his friend Benjamin Franklin worked on the book that later became the American Protestants' *Book of Common Prayer.*

'I BELIEVE THIS IS THE FIRST CHURCH WHICH HAS EVER BEEN BUILT FOR A PROSPECT (GOOD VIEW),' THE POLITICIAN JOHN WILKES TOLD SIR FRANCIS APPROVINGLY.

WOBURN ABBEY

ike so many of its kind, Woburn began as a Cistercian abbey, only to be confiscated by Henry VIII. His son gave the land to one of Henry's courtiers, the Earl of Bedford, who had lost an eye to an arrow in a raid against France. The house was rebuilt in the 17th century and now looks very grand, boasting 14 state apartments and enough art – Rembrandt, Van Dyke, Velasquez, Canaletto – to fill a museum. Yet it was suffering so badly from dry rot 50 years ago that half of it had to be pulled down. So great indeed was the mess inherited by the 13th Duke of Bedford that he was forced to turn the estate into an amusement park in 1955 and open it to the public. Other stately home owners criticised him unmercifully at the time, but many have since had no option but to follow suit.

WITH ONLY HALF OF IT LEFT, WOBURN STILL LOOKS IMPRESSIVE ENOUGH. THE LIONS AND ELEPHANTS OF THE SAFARI PARK ARE KEPT WELL AWAY FROM THE MAIN HOUSE.

CHAPTER SEVEN

THE NORTH MIDLANDS

THE INDUSTRIAL HEARTLAND

A horse! A horse! My kingdom for a horse!' One of Shakespeare's most famous lines, from the last act of *Richard III*, when the battle of Bosworth was already lost and King Richard was leading one final desperate charge to try and kill Henry Tudor before his army melted away. He failed, and was hacked to death instead. His body was stripped naked and publicly displayed in Leicester for two days, so that everyone would know he was dead. It was a fitting end for a man who thought nothing of beheading his closest friends or murdering his own nephews in the Tower.

The site of Richard's last stand lies a couple of miles south of Market Bosworth, a sleepy Midlands town more important in 1485 than now. Nobody knows the exact disposition of the rival forces, but stray cannon balls are sometimes unearthed on Glebe Farm and the western slope of Ambion Hill, which suggests that this was the position of Richard's army. The boggy ground which inconvenienced both sides is still there, albeit better drained today; and Richard's well, where he is supposed to have had a last drink before charging to his death, can still be seen below Ambion Hill.

'FURTHER SOUTH LIES CROWN HILL, NEAR STOKE GOLDING, WHERE RICHARD'S CROWN IS SAID TO HAVE BEEN RETRIEVED FROM A THORN BUSH AND PRESENTED TO HENRY TUDOR, NOW KING HENRY VII.'

Further south lies Crown Hill, near Stoke Golding, where Richard's crown is said to have been retrieved from a thorn bush and presented to Henry Tudor, now King Henry VII. The crown is supposed to have been hidden by a looter, hoping to recover it later. But it is hard to imagine how anybody could make off with such a highly visible object, even in the heat of battle.

Elsewhere, Leicestershire is a fairly unremarkable county, sitting on the edge of the coalfields and manufacturing areas of the Industrial Revolution. A new seam of coal was recently discovered underneath Belvoir Castle (once owned by Lord de Ros, who backed the wrong side in the Wars of the Roses and was beheaded for his pains). The present owner, the Duke of Rutland, threatened to throw himself

AFTER REMODELLING CHATSWORTH'S GARDENS, SIR JOSEPH PAXTON WENT ON TO DESIGN THE CRYSTAL PALACE FOR THE GREAT EXHIBITION OF 1851.

in front of the bulldozers if ever the coal was mined, and so far it hasn't been.

A few miles away lies Woolsthorpe Manor, a relatively modest house where Sir Isaac Newton spent his childhood. It was at Woolsthorpe that the idea of gravity came to him, and there are still apple trees growing in the garden where he sat.

To the north lies Lincoln, a beautiful old town with a castle, a magnificent cathedral, and the only Roman gateway in Britain still being used by traffic. And to the west is Nottingham, now a substantial manufacturing town, but best known to millions all over the world as the place where Robin Hood and Maid Marian had their contretemps with King John and the Sheriff.

Robin Hood never actually existed, so far as anyone has been able to establish, but it makes a wonderful story nevertheless. King John was left in charge of Nottingham Castle while his brother Richard the Lionheart was away at the Crusades, and is known to have behaved disgracefully. On one occasion he held 28 Welsh boys hostage as security for the good behaviour of their chieftain fathers. When the fathers showed signs of rebellion, he hanged all 28 from the castle walls. It was this kind of behaviour that lost him the support of the people and gave rise to the legend of Robin Hood.

'A FEW MILES AWAY LIES WOOLSTHORPE MANOR, A RELATIVELY MODEST HOUSE WHERE SIR ISAAC NEWTON SPENT HIS CHILDHOOD.'

The castle is still there, where King John and the shire reeve held court. It was built by William the Conqueror and was a Yorkist stronghold during the Wars of the Roses. Charles I raised his standard there to begin the Civil War in 1642. But the building fell into disuse thereafter and was sold for a private house before being destroyed by an angry mob during the Reform Bill riots of 1831.

Today it belongs to Nottingham Corporation and is used as a museum and art gallery. The rock on which it stands is riddled with caves and ancient tunnels. There is even a crusading inn – the *Trip to Jerusalem* – built into the cliff face. There is also a secret passage known as Mortimer's Hole, where Edward III (son of the unfortunate Edward II) sent his men to enter the castle by stealth and arrest his mother's lover, Mortimer, for high treason. Mortimer was taken to London and executed at Tyburn. He was hanged, drawn and quartered, using exactly the same grisly details as he himself had arranged years earlier for Hugh Despenser.

On from Nottingham lies Chatsworth, in Derbyshire, the seat of the Dukes of Devonshire since the early 17th century. The house looks like a palace from outside and is even more splendid within. It was built at a time when dukes could, and did, behave like the Duke of Omnium in Trollope's novels. Previous owners of Chatsworth thought nothing of straightening a bend in the river, if it suited them, or of moving an entire village to improve the view from the house. Mary, Queen of Scots, spent a long time as a prisoner in the previous house on the site, forbidden to go anywhere by her cousin Queen Elizabeth. The enclosed walk in the garden where she took her daily exercise is commemorated today as 'Queen Mary's Bower'.

On again from Chatsworth lies Church Stretton in Shropshire, site of a number of prehistoric barrows (burial grounds) and a well-defined Iron Age settlement near the golf course. Close to Stretton is the little town of Ironbridge, where the Iron Age was carried to its logical conclusion with the world's first... iron bridge. The bridge was erected in 1778 over the river Severn and is still used today, although no longer by wheeled traffic.

But Shropshire is better known for the prettiness of its houses and towns than its industrial pretensions. Prettiest of them all perhaps is Ludlow, with a main street made up entirely of 15th century houses and a castle once occupied by the two princes in the Tower (before they moved to London). Henry VIII's elder brother, Prince Arthur, died at the castle, and it was familiar also to Sir Philip Sidney, the Elizabethan soldier-poet, later killed at the battle of Zutphen.

'HENRY VIII'S ELDER BROTHER, PRINCE ARTHUR, DIED AT THE CASTLE, AND IT WAS FAMILIAR ALSO TO SIR PHILIP SIDNEY, THE ELIZABETHAN SOLDIER-POET, LATER KILLED AT THE BATTLE OF ZUTPHEN.'

Sidney himself spent some years nearby at Shrewsbury, where he was educated at Shrewsbury school, in the lee of another castle. The school still exists – Charles Darwin went there – and the town itself is one of the best preserved mediaeval centres in the country.

Beyond Shrewsbury, to the west, stands the border town of Llanymynech, half in England, half in Wales. The Romans mined copper and zinc from Llanymynech Hill, and the summit gives an excellent view of what remains of Offa's Dyke, the 8th century ditch dug by the King of Mercia to keep out Welsh marauders. In its heyday the ditch stretched from the mouth of the river Wye to the Dee, and it still more or less forms the boundary between England and Wales.

It served its purpose, for the Welsh were never much of a threat after it was dug. Once he had dealt with them, Offa went on to become a highly successful monarch by the standards of the day. He was on corresponding terms with the Pope and the Emperor Charlemagne, although Charlemagne greatly resented it when Offa thought of himself as an equal, rather than some provincial chieftain from the back of beyond. Charlemagne even broke off diplomatic relations for a while, but Offa was swift to mend his fences and good sense prevailed in the end.

LINCOLN

Uniquely among English cathedrals, Lincoln was the victim of a severe earthquake in 1185, which demolished everything except the towers (not so tall then) of the Norman west front. The rest of the cathedral had to be rebuilt from scratch, a daunting task which began in 1192 and was completed a mere 40 years later – astonishingly fast, by mediaeval standards.

Stone for the work was quarried on site, for the cathedral sits on top of a limestone hill, dominating both the old town below and the countryside around, much as Chartres does in France. Until a gale in the 16th century, the effect was even more impressive, for the central tower was topped by a huge spire, taking the total height to 524 feet – at that time, the tallest man-made structure in the world.

THE TOWN TAKES ITS NAME FROM LINDON, CELTIC FOR 'THE HILL FORT BY A POOL'. THE ROMANS LATINISED IT TO LINDUM COLONIA, FROM WHICH THE PRESENT NAME DERIVES.

CHATSWORTH

 hatsworth would have been the home of President Kennedy's sister if her husband, heir to the Duke of Devonshire, hadn't been killed in the Second World War. Instead it was inherited by his brother, now the 11th Duke. The first Duke received his dukedom as a reward for backing William of Orange against James II. He set about transforming the old Tudor house into the Chatsworth of today, driving his architect mad by redesigning bits at a time, then tearing them down and starting again if he disliked the result. As early as 1697 the house had a marble bath with hot and cold taps, as well as 10 flushing lavatories. It has always been popular with sightseers, so many in the early 19th century that they greatly annoyed the 6th Duke, peering through his private windows. After 1849, when the railway arrived, Chatsworth began to see 80,000 people every summer – a drop in the ocean, by today's standards.

CHATSWORTH'S SUPERB GARDENS ARE LARGELY THE WORK OF SIR JOSEPH PAXTON, WHO WAS THE SIXTH DUKE'S GARDENER FROM 1826. BUT THERE HAVE BEEN GARDENS HERE SINCE MARY, QUEEN OF SCOTS, WALKED THEM AS A PRISONER.

'AS EARLY AS 1697 THE HOUSE HAD A MARBLE BATH WITH HOT AND COLD TAPS, AS WELL AS 10 FLUSHING LAVATORIES.'

BOLSOVER CASTLE

The first castle at Bolsover was built by William Peverell, possibly an illegitimate descendant of William the Conqueror. The land was later acquired by the Cavendish family and it was Sir Charles Cavendish, son of Bess of Hardwick, who built a new castle on the site in the early 17th century. This was Britain's earliest 'sham' castle, built entirely for effect rather than for any practical purpose. The family also built a country house alongside and an indoor riding school for their ponies. The work was still not complete when Charles I and his wife came to visit in 1634. The masque composed by Ben Jonson for the occasion – Love's Welcome to Bolsover – is full of jokes about how the house still had the builders in.

'THE FIRST CASTLE AT BOLSOVER WAS BUILT BY WILLIAM PEVERELL, POSSIBLY AN ILLEGITIMATE DESCENDANT OF WILLIAM THE CONQUEROR.'

BELVOIR CASTLE

Soon after the Norman Conquest, William the Conqueror made a gift of the Mound and all the land that could be seen from it to his standard bearer, Robert de Todeni. De Todeni lost no time in building a castle on top of the hill and naming it Belvedere, today Belvoir. Via his descendants, the castle passed to Sir Robert Manners, whose own descendants, the Dukes of Rutland, still live there. The original castle suffered badly in the Wars of the Roses and again during the Civil War. The present structure was remodelled by James Wyatt in the early 19th century. Lady Diana Manners – Evelyn Waugh's Mrs Stitch – was a daughter of the house. But the most famous Manners of all was undoubtedly the Marquis of Granby, a popular general in the Seven Years War, who later gave his name to pubs and taverns all over the country.

(LEFT) ALTHOUGH WYATT WAS THE ARCHITECT, MUCH OF THE CASTLE'S GOTHIC LOOK WAS IMPOSED ON HIM BY THE FIFTH DUKE'S WIFE, WHO THOUGHT SHE COULD DO IT BETTER.

(FAR LEFT) IN 1751, THE CAVENDISH FAMILY STRIPPED THE LEAD FROM THE TERRACE ROOF TO BUILD A WING ON THEIR OTHER HOUSE AT WELBECK ABBEY. IT HAS BEEN A RUIN EVER SINCE.

CHAPTER EIGHT

WALES

THE LAND BEYOND THE MARCHES

 ffa's Dyke was dug to keep the Welsh out of England, but in truth it might have served just as well to keep the English out of Wales. The balance of invasions, from the Romans onwards, has always been heavily against the Welsh. The only successful intrusion the other way was made by Henry Tudor, who landed at Milford Haven in August 1485 (from exile in France), advanced rapidly towards Shrewsbury, and within a fortnight had defeated Richard III at Bosworth to become King of England and founder of an outstandingly successful mediaeval dynasty. But he was the exception, rather than the rule.

The Welsh, more traditionally, have been a subdued people, much given to quarrelling among themselves, and consequently much put upon by their Anglo-Saxon neighbours. Even the name Wales comes from the Anglo-Saxon for foreigners. Up until the Norman conquest, the country was divided into four principalities, each with its own agenda, each struggling for supremacy over its neighbours. After the conquest, William established three 'marcher' lordships along the Welsh marches (border), appointing the earls of Chester, Shrewsbury and Hereford to contain the Welsh and bring them under Norman domination.

'UP UNTIL THE NORMAN CONQUEST, THE COUNTRY WAS DIVIDED INTO FOUR PRINCIPALITIES, EACH WITH ITS OWN AGENDA, EACH STRUGGLING FOR SUPREMACY OVER ITS NEIGHBOURS.'

The marcher lords pursued this policy with vigour. Over a number of years, they overran southern Wales and scattered the Welsh resistance into the hills. They strengthened their grip on the new territory (to which William had no legitimate claim) by establishing a chain of motte and bailey castles from Milford Haven to the river Wye. Pembroke, Carmarthen and Caerphilly castles were all begun at this time or soon after. Other strongholds followed, other invasions as well. The Welsh were never completely conquered, but they were never completely free either. Edward I effectively ended their aspirations with the execution in 1282 of the Welsh leader Dafydd (grandson of Llewelyn the Great and brother of Llewelyn the Last) and the appointment in 1301 of his own son to the newly restored title of Prince of Wales. Thereafter the Welsh remained in a

HARLECH CASTLE WAS BUILT IN THE 13TH CENTRUY, ON A ROCKY CLIFF FACE, 200 FEET ABOVE TREMADOC BAY BUT THE SEA HAS RECEDED SO FAR SINCE THAT THE CASTLE SEEMS MAROONED INLAND. IT WAS ONE OF NINE FORTRESSES PLANNED BY EDWARD I TO CONSOLIDATE HIS HOLD ON NORTH WALES.

state of subjugation, apart from a few minor skirmishes, until the rise of Owen Glendower, their great national hero, at the beginning of the 15th century.

Glendower was a Welsh nobleman, of royal blood. Initially friendly towards the English, he had fought for Richard II and served as a courtier in London. But a dispute over land, badly handled by the English, had alienated him and in 1400 he raised his standard against the king. The Welsh flocked to his side while the English, preoccupied elsewhere, were powerless to prevent them. Glendower declared himself Prince of Wales and entered into negotiations with the Scots, Irish and French. He formed an alliance with the Duke of Northumberland, whose son Hotpsur was killed near Shrewsbury while riding to Glendower's aid. For eight years he successfully defied the English, until times changed and they were able to turn their full weight against him. In 1408 Prince Henry (later Henry V) invaded Wales, taking first Aberystwyth, then Harlech castle.

'THE WARS OF THE ROSES SAW A FURTHER LONG PERIOD OF UNREST, ALTHOUGH THE OUTCOME WAS HIGHLY SATISFACTORY TO THE WELSH, FULFILLING AS IT DID AN ANCIENT PROPHECY THAT A WELSHMAN (HENRY TUDOR, LATER HENRY VII) WOULD ONE DAY OCCUPY THE ENGLISH THRONE.'

Glendower was defeated and forced into hiding. He disappeared in 1412 and died four years later, in a place unknown, having made no response to Henry's repeated offers of a royal pardon.

Glendower left the Welsh with a renewed pride in themselves, but in no shape to resist the English any further. The Wars of the Roses saw a further long period of unrest, although the outcome was highly satisfactory to the Welsh, fulfilling as it did an ancient prophecy that a Welshman (Henry Tudor, later Henry VII) would one day occupy the English throne. In 1535 his son, Henry VIII, signed the Act of Union that abolished the powers of the marcher lords and made the Welsh, if not equal partners with the English, then at least not foreigners either.

Henceforth they returned members to the English parliament and enjoyed access to the English professions and armed services. The two legal systems were gradually harmonised until the Welsh had been more or less totally absorbed by the English. They were also forced to speak the English language, but it could be argued that this did them more good than harm, in the long run.

Under the Stuart kings, the Welsh enjoyed less favour at court, although they remained predominantly Royalist during the Civil War. The war itself affected them relatively little, Wales being of no strategic value to the warring parties. Harlech castle was besieged again, and Pembroke castle (held first for Parliament and then for the King) took a considerable pounding from artillery before lack of water forced the garrison to surrender. For the most part though, the Welsh remained little more than bemused onlookers while the real fighting was done elsewhere. And since the Civil War, they have always been at peace with themselves and their neighbours.

The legacy of their history is a formidable array of ancient castles, not only in south Wales, but also in the north and along the marches, where - Offa's Dyke notwithstanding - the exact position of the border with England was always in dispute. Beaumaris is a splendid example, and so are Caernarvon and Cilgerran (painted by Turner). At Hawarden there are two castles, one an ancient fortress 'slighted' during the Civil War, the other an 18th century country house, home for more than 50 years of William Ewart Gladstone. Throughout his political career, the Grand Old Man always made a point of spending at least six months of every year at Hawarden, arguing that running a country or balancing the national budget were really only the problems of estate management writ large.

'THE LEGACY OF THEIR HISTORY IS A FORMIDABLE ARRAY OF ANCIENT CASTLES, NOT ONLY IN SOUTH WALES, BUT ALSO IN THE NORTH AND ALONG THE MARCHES, WHERE — OFFA'S DYKE NOTWITHSTANDING — THE EXACT POSITION OF THE BORDER WITH ENGLAND WAS ALWAYS IN DISPUTE.'

So attached were the Gladstone family to Wales that during the First World War William's grandson, himself a Member of Parliament, chose to serve in a Welsh regiment rather than one of the more fashionable English ones. So too did Sir Clough Williams-Ellis, a distinguished architect, who became one of the first officers in the newly formed Welsh Guards. The young Gladstone was killed on the Western front, but Williams-Ellis survived to devote his life to architecture, and in particular to the building of an extraordinary Mediterranean village on the shores of Tremadog bay.

Inspired by a visit to Portofino, he set out to create at Portmeirion an Italianate village of a kind Wales - or England, for that matter - had never seen before. The result was an eclectic mix of Romanesque, Baroque and 'light opera', often incorporating old bits and pieces from ruined stately homes in the neighbourhood. If Walt Disney or William Randolph Hearst had done the same in America, the British would have recoiled in horror. As it is however, they have taken Portmeirion to their hearts, even though, in architectural terms, the village is eccentric in the extreme. So eccentric in fact that it was used as the setting for the 1960s TV drama *The Prisoner*, starring Patrick McGoohan, and is still visited by thousands of fans from all over the world who might otherwise never think of going to Wales at all.

'THE CASTLE PASSED TO THE DESPENSER FAMILY IN 1317 AND SHELTERED THE HAPLESS EDWARD II FOR A WHILE, AS WELL AS OWEN GLENDOWER IN THE EARLY 1400S.'

CAERPHILLY CASTLE

 aerphilly, in mid-Glamorgan, is the country's first concentric castle, the model for those later built by Edward I. It was begun by Gilbert de Clare, Earl of Gloucester, in 1268, only to be destroyed by Llewelyn the Last in 1270. But de Clare began again a year later, though still under siege by Llewelyn. Caerphilly is noted for its formidable outer defences, with a strong outwork to the west and a 1000 foot protective dam to the east, making it in area the second largest castle in the country after Windsor. The castle passed to the Despenser family in 1317 and sheltered the hapless Edward II for a while, as well as Owen Glendower in the early 1400s. It lost its purpose after the subjugation of the Welsh and was already in decay by the mid-16th century. Oliver Cromwell tried to blow up one of the drum towers, which remains at a drunken angle to this day.

THE MOAT FORMED AN INTEGRAL PART OF THE CASTLE'S EXCEPTIONALLY ELABORATE DEFENCES. SO THE ROUNDHEADS DID THE OBVIOUS THING IN THE CIVIL WAR: THEY DRAINED IT.

TINTERN ABBEY

tanding quietly on the banks of the Wye, Tintern was torn apart during the Dissolution of the Monasteries and has remained uninhabited ever since. The abbey was founded by Cistercians from Normandy in 1131, and took a century and a half to build. Cistercians always preferred to build in open countryside, rather than close to a town, which explains why Tintern's layout is grander than most. But the monks were expelled in 1536 and the property given to the Earl of Worcester, who stripped the lead from the roofs and used it elsewhere, probably on the castles at Raglan and Chepstow. The abbey lay in ruins thereafter, but has never lost its romantic appeal. It was particularly popular with tourists in the 18th and 19th centuries – Wordsworth among them – who travelled long distances to come and see it.

HOW OFT, IN SPIRIT, HAVE I TURNED TO THEE
  O SYLVAN WYE! THOU WANDERER THROUGH THE WOOD
  HOW OFTEN HAS MY SPIRIT TURNED TO THEE!

WORDSWORTH
LINES WRITTEN A FEW MILES ABOVE TINTERN ABBEY

PORTMEIRION

est known to TV viewers as the setting for the cult series *The Prisoner*, Portmeirion is thoroughly surreal in concept – an Italianate village on the coast of Wales, all Mediterranean exuberance under a leaden sky. It was the brainchild of Sir Clough Williams-Ellis, who came home from Portofino determined to create something similar on his native shore. He found the right site in 1925 and spent the next 50 years building his dream village on the cliff leading down to the sea. All sorts of different materials were used – panelling from a Flintshire banqueting hall, sandstone colonnades from Bristol, an enormous Buddha from a film set – whatever came to hand. The result is a hodgepodge of architectural styles, but highly imaginative and great fun.

WILLIAMS-ELLIS ONCE CALLED PORTMEIRION A 'HOME FOR FALLEN BUILDINGS', WHICH IS MORE OR LESS WHAT IT IS.

PEMBROKE CASTLE

oins from Roman times have been found at Pembroke, but the first serious fortification – 'a slender fortress of stakes and turf' – was built at the end of the 11th century. It was replaced in the 13th by the present stone structure, one of a chain of Norman strongpoints for the domination of Wales. Henry Tudor, later Henry VII, was born in the castle in 1457, 'this day of St Agnes, that I did bring into this world my good and gracious prince,' as his 13-year-old mother proclaimed. The castle was held by the Roundheads during the Civil War, until the military governor changed his mind and sided with the King. It was then bombarded for 48 days until lack of water forced the garrison to surrender. The castle was slighted and its stones used as a quarry for the next 200 years, before being restored in this century.

THE ROOM WHERE THE
FUTURE HENRY VII WAS
BORN CAN STILL BE SEEN, IN
THE DRUM-TOWER NEXT TO
THE GATEHOUSE.

CHAPTER NINE

THE NORTH
VIKING COUNTRY

he Vikings managed to penetrate most parts of England during the wave of invasions that took place in the 9th and 10th centuries, but it was in the north of England, especially the eastern seaboard, that their presence was most strongly felt. Even today, their influence in the north can be seen in all sorts of ways, from the Ridings (administrative areas) of Yorkshire, to towns with names like Hunmanby and Skelmanthorpe, to the Nordic blood group enjoyed by most of the British population north of the Wash. When British football hooligans follow their teams to Copenhagen or Oslo for an international match, they even go 'berserk' in the streets, a performance not often appreciated by the people who coined the term in the first place.

The Danes are peaceful now, but it was not always so. When they came to the Holy Island of Lindisfarne in 883, peace was the last thing on their minds. They sacked the monastery and laid waste everything in their path. Fortunately, the monks fled inland, taking the coffin of St Cuthbert with them. A hundred and twenty years later, still with the coffin, they arrived at Durham, where a steeply wooded bend in the river provided a formidable obstacle against attack. Here Durham castle was built and Durham cathedral, as a shrine to the saint.

'MORE THAN ANY OTHER NORTHERN CITY, YORK HAS PLAYED A PART IN EVERY GENERATION OF ENGLISH HISTORY, FROM THE ROMANS — CONSTANTINE THE GREAT WAS PROCLAIMED EMPEROR THERE — TO THE GERMAN BOMBINGS OF THE 20TH CENTURY.'

Equally impressive as a cathedral city is York, known as Jorvik to the Vikings, who used it as their English capital for almost 100 years. More than any other northern city, York has played a part in every generation of English history, from the Romans — Constantine the Great was proclaimed emperor there — to the German bombings of the 20th century. The core of the city is still mediaeval: the Minster, the building nearby where Richard III proclaimed his son Prince of Wales, the city gates where the heads of traitors were impaled, the huge defensive walls, later breached by Roundheads attacking the Royalists within. It is quite possible to stand where Richard did and look at buildings that have hardly changed at all since his time. Possible too to stand with the Royalists as they

DURHAM CASTLE, BUILT BY THE NORMANS AFTER THE REBELLION OF 1069, IS DWARFED BY THE CATHEDRAL, BUILT A FEW YEARS LATER.

fought the Roundheads and pushed them back through the walls. Few English cities, if any, make it so easy for the imagination to travel back in time.

As with other parts of the country, the north is also well supplied with castles, often, as in York's case, providing the nucleus for a city's defences, but sometimes standing alone, perched on rocky headlands facing out to a hostile sea. Lindisfarne was heavily restored at the beginning of the 20th century, but Bamburgh can trace its origins to a wooden fortress built on top of the 150 foot cliff in the year 547. Alnwick, in Northumberland, is still occupied by the Percy family (Shakespeare's Hotspur), who acquired the Norman castle in 1309. The battlements are studded with stone figures, 18th century replacements for the stone sentries put there in the Middle Ages to confuse enemy spies. The deception was carefully organised, but did not always work out. In 1596 for example, a party of Scots raided the castle and bypassed the statues altogether, tying up the real sentries before escaping with all their horses.

'LINDISFARNE WAS HEAVILY RESTORED AT THE BEGINNING OF THE 20TH CENTURY, BUT BAMBURGH CAN TRACE ITS ORIGINS TO A WOODEN FORTRESS BUILT ON TOP OF THE 150 FOOT CLIFF IN THE YEAR 547.'

Other castles in the north were built more for decorative purposes than for defence. One that ought to be mentioned is Castle Howard, in Yorkshire, which is not really a castle at all, although built on the site of one. Rather it is a country house, very grand, designed by Sir John Vanbrugh (who also designed Blenheim Palace) with a flamboyance that was revolutionary for its time and has only rarely been emulated. Television viewers will remember it as the ancestral home of Sebastian Flyte in *Brideshead Revisited*.

But Yorkshire is not really Evelyn Waugh country, or even Vanbrugh's, who was a noted playwright. In literary terms, it belongs to the Brontë family, if it belongs to anyone. Haworth parsonage, where the authors of *Jane Eyre* and *Wuthering Heights* grew up, has changed little since their time, although the church has been almost completely rebuilt. The town is industrial and grim, as it was then, and the moors beyond are as bleak as ever. Haworth is often a disappointment to tourists, whose diet of glossy book covers leads them to expect something more romantic, but it remains the second most popular literary shrine after Stratford. Visitors often forget that the Brontës took to writing, as many authors do, to escape the ugliness of their everyday surroundings.

Many authors, but not all. Northwest of Haworth lies Grasmere, in the Lake

Disrict, where Wordsworth lived for much of his life, first at Dove Cottage, later at Allan Bank. Neither home is distinguished; nor is the town. But the setting, on the edge of the lake, below Helm Crag and Nab Scar, is as beautiful as anywhere in England – 'the loveliest spot that man hath ever found', as the poet himself put it. Coleridge agreed, as did Southey and de Quincey. Between them, they lived in the Lake District for many years, often in each other's houses, doing most of their best work there.

Elsewhere, this part of England is an uneasy mixture of sweeping landscape and industrial sprawl, a legacy of its role as the cradle of the industrial revolution. The world's first railway ran from Stockton to Darlington, where a portion of the original track is preserved at Bank Top station, alongside George Stephenson's Locomotion Number One engine. Coal for the new service, indeed for the entire revolution, came from the abundant coal fields of Durham and Yorkshire. The colliery village of Washington, in county Durham, was typical of many, an ugly place, made up largely of pit-head buildings and rows of cheaply built terraces for the miners.

'THE WORLD'S FIRST RAILWAY RAN FROM STOCKTON TO DARLINGTON, WHERE A PORTION OF THE ORIGINAL TRACK IS PRESERVED AT BANK TOP STATION, ALONGSIDE GEORGE STEPHENSON'S LOCOMOTION NUMBER ONE engine.'

Much of Washington has been reconstructed now, but the mediaeval Old Hall still stands near the town centre. The Washington family were lords of the manor there from 1183 to 1376, when they moved south to Sulgrave in Northamptonshire. Later still, a branch of the family emigrated to America, taking with them their coat of arms – three stars and two stripes. When the time came to design a flag for the newly United States, it seemed only natural to incorporate the Washington arms into it, as a mark of respect for the country's first President and Father of the Nation. Today, those arms of a minor English squire must rank as one of the best known symbols in the entire world – and indeed the moon, where a US flag still marks the spot where Neil Armstrong made his giant leap for mankind in 1969.

YORK

ittle changed since Richard III worshipped there, the ancient minster is the jewel in York's crown, second in importance only to Canterbury cathedral in Kent. The minster was built between 1220 and 1470 on the site of an earlier church much damaged by fire in 1137. Some of its stained glass windows are 800 years old, but the bulk of the minster is mediaeval rather than Norman. So too are the city's formidable walls, rebuilt in the 13th century. The Micklegate, through which all reigning monarchs traditionally enter the city, has been there since at least Norman times. The head of Sir Henry Percy (Shakespeare's Hotspur) was displayed on a spike over the gate, as was the Duke of York's in 1460, surmounted by a crown of rushes to mock his royal pretensions.

'SOME OF ITS STAINED GLASS WINDOWS ARE 800 YEARS OLD, BUT THE BULK OF THE MINSTER IS MEDIAEVAL RATHER THAN NORMAN.'

ADVANCING NORTH IN AD 71, THE ROMANS ESTABLISHED A FORT AT THE POINT WHERE THE RIVER OUSE MET THE FOSS. THEY CALLED IT EBORACUM, TODAY YORK.

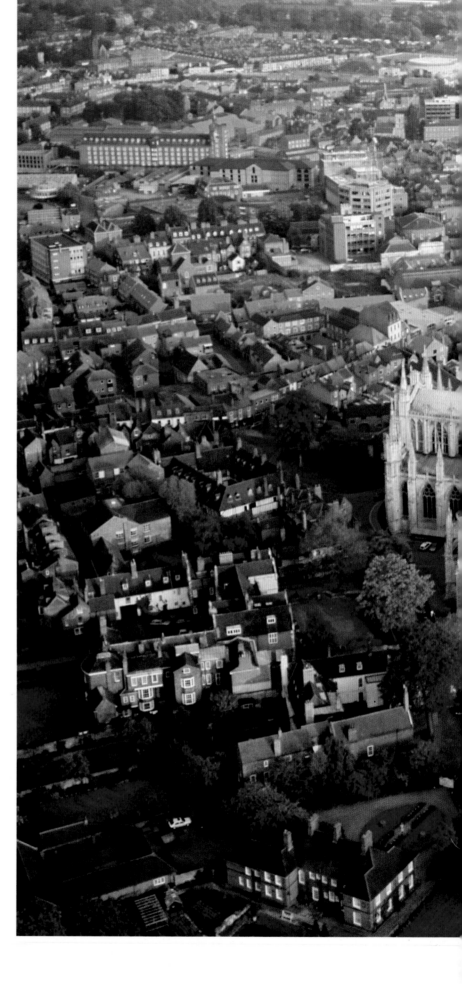

HADRIAN'S WALL

adrian's Wall marks the northernmost point of the Roman Empire in Britain. Beyond it lay Caledonia, land of Picts, Scots and other hill tribes, impossible to control or subdue. Rather than invade the Scottish Highlands, which were of little economic importance, the emperor Hadrian built a wall instead, to confine the barbarians within their own boundaries, where they could do no harm. Work began around 122 AD and was completed some time after 130. The wall ran 73 miles, from Wallsend on one side of England to the Solway Firth on the other. On average it was seven feet thick and perhaps 15 tall, protected by a total of 17 forts at regular intervals. Most of it has disappeared now, but there are still places where one can see what life must have been like for a Roman soldier at the furthest outpost of the empire, almost 2000 years ago.

THE WALL WAS BUILT AFTER THE ROMANS' NINTH LEGION SET OFF TO QUELL A REBELLION AND WAS NEVER HEARD OF AGAIN.

LINDISFARNE PRIORY

 n a cheerless January morning in 793, a group of unfamiliar sails appeared in the mist just off the Northumbrian coast. The sails belonged to a Viking fleet, on its way to attack the abbey on the Holy Island of Lindisfarne. The monks were overrun before help could reach them from the mainland. Many were killed, the remainder taken away to be sold as slaves. Cattle were taken too, and a fortune in gold and jewels. The entire island was laid waste, in an episode that horrified all of Christian Europe. It marked the beginning of more than 200 years of Viking rampaging along the English coast. The ruins of the priory (left) date from the 11th century and replaced the abbey destroyed by the Vikings.

LINDISFARNE IS ONLY AN ISLAND AT HIGH TIDE. A THREE MILE CAUSEWAY CONNECTS IT TO THE MAINLAND FOR THE SIX HOURS OF LOW TIDE.

DURHAM

tanding on a horseshoe bend of the river Wear, Durham's steeply wooded slopes have always been a strong deterrent against attack. The castle at the landward end of the horseshoe was built immediately after the Norman Conquest, and the cathedral was begun a few years later. It houses the bones of St Cuthbert, an early missionary in northern England. He was buried first at Lindisfarne, off the Northumbrian coast. But Viking raids forced the monks of the priory to flee with his coffin. They wandered for 120 years before settling in Durham in 997. The venerable Bede is buried in the cathedral too. The knocker on the great north door still boasts the ring that gave sanctuary in the Middle Ages to anyone who touched it, including – according to the list in the sanctuary book – a great many vagabonds and murderers.

THE CURFEW IMPOSED ON DURHAM, AFTER A REBELLION IN 1069, STILL RINGS EVERY WEEKDAY EVENING AT 9 P.M.

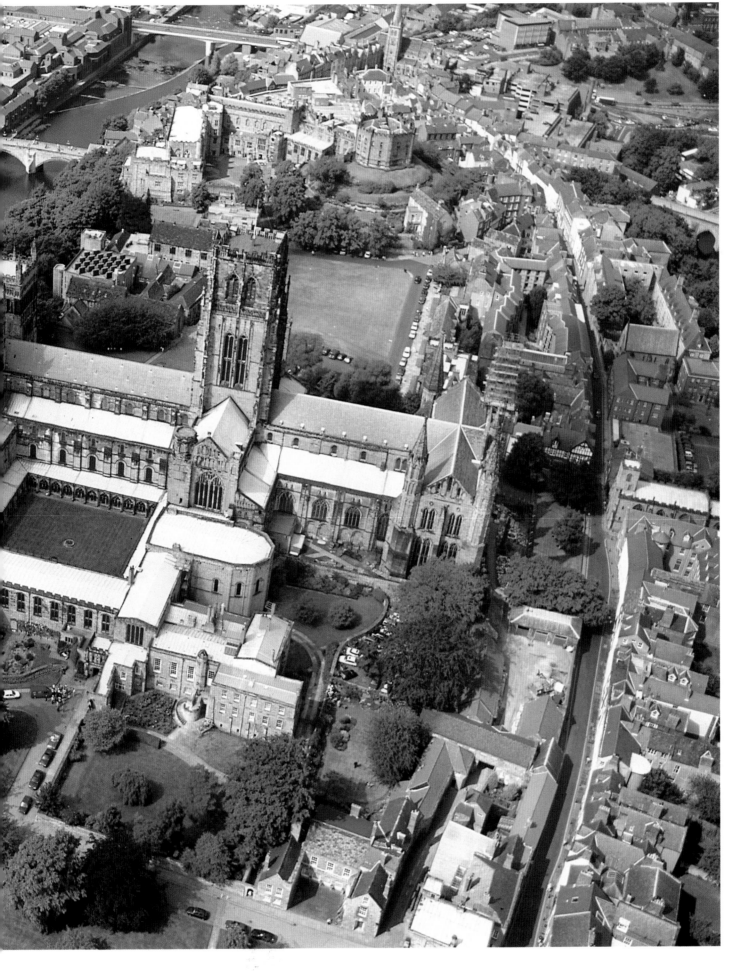

'THE KNOCKER ON THE GREAT NORTH DOOR STILL BOASTS THE RING THAT GAVE SANCTUARY IN THE MIDDLE AGES TO ANYONE WHO TOUCHED IT, INCLUDING — ACCORDING TO THE LIST IN THE SANCTUARY BOOK — A GREAT MANY VAGABONDS AND MURDERERS.'

CHAPTER TEN

SCOTLAND

A NATION UNTO ITSELF

he Scots are, and always have been, a very different people to the English. There is a tendency south of the border to assume that any Scotsman who has been successful in life – and the Scots have produced more than their share of famous men – is really only an Englishman in disguise. Speak for example of Dr Livingstone, James Watt, Alexander Fleming, John Logie Baird, John Dunlop (who invented the pneumatic tyre), John Macadam (who invented tarmac), and the English will blithely assume that these are all Englishmen. That they all came from north of Hadrian's Wall is, so far as the English are concerned, beside the point.

The Scots of course see it quite differently. They are a fiercely independent nation, with a very strong identity of their own. They have never been successfully conquered, although they have sometimes been defeated in battle. The Romans beat them in the Lowlands, but declined to pursue them into their mountain retreats. The English beat them as well, on occasion, but only with help from the Scots themselves. When the two countries came together in the Act of Union of 1707, it was not an act of English imperialism but a voluntary agreement between two sovereign states, albeit with considerable misgivings on the Scottish side. The Scots lost their Parliament under the Act, but they insisted on retaining their own laws, their own customs, their own bank notes – even their own language, for those who continued to speak it. They remained separate as a cultural entity, and still do today.

They were Picts and Celts originally, augmented in the 6th century AD by an infusion of Gaels from Ireland, in the 9th by Vikings from Denmark and Norway. A number of English settled in Scotland as well, after the Norman invasion, for William never conquered north of the border and the Norman imposition of feudalism never took serious hold there. The Scots in the Highlands remained impregnable, continuing to speak Gaelic long after their Lowland brothers had succumbed first to Norman French, then to English. In the Orkney and Shetlands they didn't even speak Gaelic, but clung to their Norse heritage

'THEY ARE A FIERCELY INDEPENDENT NATION, WITH A VERY STRONG IDENTITY OF THEIR OWN.'

ACROSS THE VALLEY FROM STIRLING CASTLE, ON TOP OF ABBEY CRAIG, STANDS THE MONUMENT TO SIR WILLIAM WALLACE, ONE OF SCOTLAND'S MOST FAMOUS SONS.

until late in the 15th century, when a Danish princess married James III and brought the islands with her as part of her dowry.

The history of such a diverse people has inevitably been turbulent. The Romans, who had conquered the rest of Britain with relative ease, found them very difficult to deal with. In AD 118, the Roman Governor sent a legion to Scotland to quell a rebellion. The legion set off for the Highlands and was never heard of again. The 9th legion simply vanished into the Scottish mist, leaving no trace behind it – an episode that has puzzled historians ever since. Soon afterwards, the Emperor Hadrian ordered a wall to be built from one side of England to the other, to contain the Scots and keep them within their boundaries. From the stretches of the wall that survive today, it is clear that the Romans took the work very seriously indeed – a painful admission of failure perhaps, from what was then the most powerful military nation on earth.

'SOON AFTERWARDS, THE EMPEROR HADRIAN ORDERED A WALL TO BE BUILT FROM ONE SIDE OF ENGLAND TO THE OTHER, TO CONTAIN THE SCOTS AND KEEP THEM WITHIN THEIR BOUNDARIES.'

Subsequent rulers found the Scots no easier. The first monarch of any lasting interest was Macbeth, a contemporary of King Canute in England, who reigned for 17 years after murdering King Duncan in 1040. Lady Macbeth, the infamous schemer of Shakespeare's play, was the great niece of a man murdered by an earlier Scottish king, and thus had rather more claim to the throne than Shakespeare allowed her. Macbeth too was a wiser ruler than he was painted. Scotland enjoyed years of relative prosperity under his leadership, until his past caught up with him and he was killed by Duncan's son in August 1057.

Scotland's history thereafter was very much a mirror image of England's in the same period – a shifting battleground of uneasy alliances and constant intrigue as warlords struggled for the crown. The Scots remember two men in particular from this time: William Wallace, who rallied the Scots in 1297 to drive the English out of the Lowlands; and Robert the Bruce, who led the Scottish army at Bannockburn in 1314, when a far superior English army was routed after Bruce had personally killed the English champion, Sir Henry de Bohun, in single combat. The defeated English had little choice but to concede independence to Scotland, and so it remained until the Act of Union almost 400 years later.

Relations continued to be uneasy however, largely because of the Auld Alliance – a long-lasting association between Scotland and France, which the English always regarded with deep suspicion. When Mary, Queen of Scots, married the French Dauphin in 1558, relations between the two countries became so close that Mary even made a will bequeathing Scotland to France if she died without an heir. But the Dauphin died first and Mary returned alone to Scotland. There, her son by her second marriage succeeded her as James VI of Scotland and later, after Mary's cousin Elizabeth had died childless, James I of England.

But the Scots were never a success on the English throne. James's son, Charles I, provoked the country to civil war and was duly executed in 1649. Charles's son, James II, narrowly escaped the same fate before fleeing to France, where he later died in exile. His heirs twice attempted to reclaim the crown on their own behalf – the rebellions of 1715 and 1745 – but without success. After that, the Scots abandoned their support for the Jacobites and came grudgingly to terms with the idea of a German Protestant on the throne. The English assisted by recruiting disaffected Scottish regiments into the British army, a process which led to a gradual reconciliation between the two nations. But it was not until the 20th century, when a Scottish earl's daughter married George VI and gave birth to the present Queen Elizabeth, that a monarch has again sat on the throne who could be considered even remotely Scottish.

'SO DISTINGUISHED IS EDINBURGH, BOTH ACADEMICALLY AND ARCHITECTURALLY, THAT ITS CITIZENS HAVE ALWAYS THOUGHT OF IT PROUDLY AS THE ATHENS OF THE NORTH.'

The aristocracy, on the other hand, have always been Scottish, and every bit as ancient as their English counterparts. Glamis and Cawdor were familiar names in Macbeth's time, familiar still today. Scottish peers tend also to be clan chiefs, direct descendants of the Highland warriors who led their people into battle. The Duke of Atholl, chief of the Murrays, still maintains a private army, the only person besides the Queen allowed to do so. Those peers who can afford it continue to live in their ancestral castles, many of which were remodelled in the 18th and 19th centuries into the romantic style known as Scottish baronial. Glamis is a good example, and Inverary, and the Duke of Roxburgh's home at Floors.

The intelligentsia too have always been completely independent. By the 18th century, it was to Edinburgh that the high fliers went, rather than to Oxford or Cambridge. The Scottish Enlightenment peaked at the end of the 18th century, but the Scots have remained at the forefront of intellectual thinking ever since. So distinguished is Edinburgh, both academically and architecturally, that its citizens have always thought of it proudly as the Athens of the North. The English in their turn call it the Reykyavik of the South, which only goes to show, in the opinion of the Scots, that the English, as so often, simply don't know what they're talking about.

EDINBURGH CASTLE

 erched on a cliff almost 300 feet above the city, the castle began life as Edwin's burgh, a wooden fortress built in the 7th century by the King of Northumbria. The oldest surviving part of it is St Margaret's chapel, dating from the 11th century. The castle seems impregnable at first glance, but in fact has been captured many times. Robert the Bruce's army took it by an assault directly up the rock face, Sir William Douglas by disguising a dozen Highlanders as merchants and persuading the porter to open the gates. Oliver Cromwell besieged the castle for only 12 days before negotiating a surrender. The castle has not seen any action since, although Bonnie Prince Charlie did make a half-hearted attempt to capture it in 1745.

'THE CASTLE SEEMS IMPREGNABLE AT FIRST GLANCE, BUT IN FACT HAS BEEN CAPTURED MANY TIMES.'

AFTER RICCIO'S MURDER AT HOLYROOD, MARY, QUEEN OF SCOTS, MOVED TO EDINBURGH CASTLE TO GIVE BIRTH TO HER SON, LATER JAMES I OF ENGLAND. THE ROOM STILL EXISTS.

HOLYROOD HOUSE

ooking across Edinburgh towards the castle, Holyroodhouse takes its name from the 'holy rood' – a piece of Christ's cross – bequeathed by St Margaret of Scotland to her son David. The palace was originally the guest house for a monastery, greatly enlarged in later years. Mary, Queen of Scots, lived in the James IV tower, and it was there that she kept court with her Italian musician, David Riccio, and other Catholic favourites. On 9 March 1566, she was having supper with them when a group of Scottish nobles burst in, determined to scatter her advisers and impose a Protestant council in their place. Riccio was dragged into the next room and stabbed to death (the spot can still be seen). Mary narrowly escaped with her life, only to lose it later at the hands of her cousin Queen Elizabeth.

BONNIE PRINCE CHARLIE MADE HOLYROOD HIS HEADQUARTERS AFTER FAILING TO CAPTURE THE CASTLE AT THE OTHER END OF TOWN.

FLOORS CASTLE

ir Walter Scott called the land around Floors a 'kingdom for Oberon and Titania', which is a little hyperbolic. But there is no denying that Floors is a magnificent castle in a magnificent setting. It is the home of the Dukes of Roxburghe, the 3rd of whom amassed a superb library in the latter half of the 18th century. The books included Caxton's *Recuyell of the Historye of Troye*, a first edition of the *Decameron*, and many other treasures. But the 5th Duke was forced to sell them all in 1812 to pay a legal debt. The bulk of the collection went to his fellow aristocrats, 24 of whom formed the Roxburghe Club to keep the spirit of the collection alive. The club continues on a hereditary basis to this day.

'IT IS THE HOME OF THE DUKES OF ROXBURGHE, THE 3RD OF WHOM AMASSED A SUPERB LIBRARY IN THE LATTER HALF OF THE 18TH CENTURY.'

THE CENTRAL PART OF FLOORS DATES FROM THE 1720s, BUT THE WHOLE BUILDING WAS HEAVILY REMODELLED IN VICTORIAN TIMES.

OBAN

heltered by the island of Kerrera, off the West Highland coast, Oban seems an unlikely place for Stone Age man to have made his home. In the 19th century however, a group of workmen uncovered seven caves containing the remains of 'Azilian Man', dating from about 6000 BC. From these humble beginnings, Oban remained a modest settlement until early in the last century, when the development of farming and shipbuilding led to a rapid increase in size. Piers were built for Clyde steamboats, and the Glasgow railway arrived in 1880. McCaig's folly, on top of the hill, dates from the 1890s. The ruins of Dunollie Castle, west of the esplanade, were once the stronghold of the MacDougall family, Lords of Lorn.

(BELOW) GOLF ALMOST CERTAINLY DERIVES FROM THE DUTCH FOR A CLUB: KOLF. BUT IT HAS BEEN POPULAR IN SCOTLAND SINCE AT LEAST 1457, WHEN THE AUTHORITIES TRIED TO BAN IT.

(ABOVE) GAELIC IS STILL THE FIRST LANGUAGE FOR SOME PEOPLE IN OBAN, OFTEN ISLANDERS TRAVEL TO THE MAINLAND TO CONTINUE THEIR EDUCATION.

ST ANDREW'S

he Dutch would dispute it, but to many people in the world, St Andrew's is the birthplace of golf. The town's Royal and Ancient Golf Club was founded in 1754 and still makes the rules. In Scottish egalitarian tradition, anyone who pays a modest green fee can play, without needing an introduction or becoming a member. The golf links are visible in the distance, just beyond the buildings of the university, Scotland's oldest, founded in 1411 and still going strong. The undergraduates have a tradition of walking the harbour wall in scarlet gowns at certain times, often Sunday mornings. The east face of St Andrew's cathedral, beyond the gravestones of St Rule, is all that remains of what was once a splendid 12th century building. The castle too is in ruins. But some of the gardens in the old town, known as 'riggs', are still intact after 500 years.

URQUHART CASTLE

ith a commanding view of the loch, Urquhart Castle features in a famous photograph of the Loch Ness 'monster', taken in 1955. Scottish bank manager P.A. MacNab, on holiday with his son, was preparing to take a picture of the castle when he noticed a disturbance in the water. Hurriedly changing lenses, he photographed something long and dark, breaking the surface of the loch at between nine and 14 mph. The object submerged immediately and was never seen again. Controversy has raged ever since as to exactly what it was. The castle itself dates from the 13th century, but was blown up in 1689 in the aftermath of the Glorious Revolution (when the Catholic King James II was forcibly removed from the English throne). Its 16th century tower remains a popular viewing platform for sightseers in search of that ever elusive monster.

THE 'FEARSOME BEASTIE' OF LOCH NESS WAS FIRST RECORDED IN THE LATIN LIFE OF THE GREAT ST COLUMBA, IN 565 AD.

STIRLING CASTLE

 traddling the gateway to the Scottish Highlands, Stirling was always being besieged by one army or another during Scotland's incessant wars with the English. It is a fine natural fortress on three sides, rising sheer and stark out of the surrounding plain. It suffered its most spectacular siege in 1304, when Edward I's army attacked a tiny garrison for 12 weeks with mangonels and catapults – the most sophisticated missile-throwing devices of the day. Lead for the catapults' counterweights was stripped from church roofs for miles around. The English captured the castle then, but lost it again after their defeat at Bannockburn – two miles south – in 1314. The castle was rebuilt from the 15th century and later became a royal palace. It was besieged again by General Monck during the Civil War and by Bonnie Prince Charlie in 1745, but has lain at peace ever since.

THE CASTLE'S IMPORTANCE DECLINED AFTER 1603, WHEN JAMES VI BECAME JAMES I OF ENGLAND AND THE SCOTTISH COURT MOVED TO LONDON.

INDEX

Page numbers in *italics* indicate illustrations

Adam, Robert 54
Albert, Prince 52
Aldeburgh 85
Alfred the Great 46, 49, 71, 76
Arundel Castle *13*, 14, 22
Ashburnham, Roger 17
Astor, William Waldorf 109
Austen, Jane 49, 51, 54
Azilian man *156*

Badminton House 92
Bannockburn, battle of 90, 150, 158
Bath 49, *54-5*
Battle Abbey *25*
Belvoir Castle 116, *125*
Berkeley 92
Berkeley Castle 90, *94-5*
Bodiam Castle *27*
Boleyn, Anne 14, 38, 60, 78
Bolsover Castle *124*
Bosworth, battle of 15, 116, 126
Bradford-on-Avon *56-7*
Brightling Churchyard *28-9*
Brighton, Royal Pavilion *30-1*, 100
Bronte family 140
Brunel, Isambard Kingdom 66, 97

Caerphilly Castle *130*
Cambridge 82-4, *86-7*, 105
Canterbury 15, 142
Canute, King 49
Castle Howard 140
Cavendish, Sir Charles 124
Charles I 77, 80, 118, 151
Charles II 49, 62, 80
Charlie, Bonnie Prince 153, 158
Chartwell *33*
Chatsworth *117*, 118-19, *122-3*
Cheltenham *96*
Chequers 107
Chippendale, Thomas 71
Church Stretton 119
Churchill, Sir Winston 15, *32*

Civil War 26, 61, 68, 92, 102, 118, 125, 136, 158
Clifton Suspension Bridge 97
Cliveden *4*, 106-7, *109*
Cockerell, Samuel and Charles 100
Compton Wynyates 92
Constable, John 84-5
Cowes 58
Cromwell, Oliver 89, 131, 153
Cuthbert, St 138, 146

Dalyngrigge, Sir Edward 26
Danes 76, 138
Darby, Abraham 9
Darlington 141
Darwin, Charles 66, 119
Dashwood, Sir Francis 104-6, 112
Despenser family 90, 104, 131
Devonport 66-7
Devonshire, Dukes of 118, 122
Dickens, Charles 54, 74
Douglas, Sir William 153
Dover 12, 14
Doyle, Sir Arthur Conan 48
Drake, Sir Francis 46-8, 49, 51, 66
Dunollie Castle, Oban *156*
Durham *139*, *147*

East India Company 100
Edinburgh 151
    Castle *152*
    Holyroodhouse *154*
Edward the Confessor 76
Edward I 126, 127, 131, 158
Edward II 90, 93, 94, 104, 131
Edward III 118
Edward VII 102
Edwin, King of Northumbria 153
Elizabeth I 38, 62, 84, 107, 119, 151, 154
Elizabeth II 107, 151
Ely 82
    Cathedral *83*, 85
Eton College 105

Fielding, Henry 73
Floors Castle 151, *155*

Forde Abbey *64-5*
Fowles, John 48-9, 51
Franklin, Benjamin 106, 112
Fuller, `Mad Jack' 28

Gainsborough, Thomas 84, 85
George II 62
George IV 30
George VI 151
Gibbon, Edward 71
Glendower, Owen 126, 127, 128, 131
Granby, Marquis of 125
Grasmere 140
Great Fire 76, *77*, 79
Great Plague 76
Greenwich Observatory 36
Grey, Lady Jane 78

Hadlow Castle 15, *34-5*
Hadrian's Wall *144*, 150
Hardy, Thomas 48
Harlech Castle *127*, 128
Harold, King 12-14, 24
Hastings, battle of 12-14, 24
Hatfield 107
Haworth 140
Heath, Edward 58, 73
Hellfire Club 104-6, 112
Henley *108*
Henry I 60
Henry II 124
Henry V 60, 127, 128
Henry VI 78, 82, 86, 105
Henry VII 15, 116, 126, 127, 128, 136
Henry VIII 14, 20, 23, 24, 38, 58, 60, 64, 80, 114, 128
Hereward the Wake 82
Herstmonceux Castle *36-7*
Hever Castle 14, *38-9*
Hoare, Sir Henry 71
Holyroodhouse 154
Howard, Catherine 23, 78

Ickworth *88*
Ightham Mote 7, 15, *20-1*
Industrial Revolution 9
Ironbridge *9*, 119

Jack the Ripper 77
James I 80, 151
James II 49, 51, 64, 72, 122, 151, 157
James III of Scotland 150

James, Henry 15, 18
John, King 60, 118
Julius Caesar 12

Knole 15, *40*

Lake District 140-1
Leeds Castle 14
Lichfield, battle of 102
Lincoln 118
    Cathedral *120-1*
Lindisfarne 138, 140, *145*, 146
Llanmynech 119
London 74-7
    Banqueting Hall 77, *80*
    Downing Street *81*
    Foreign Office *81*
    Horse Guards *80*
    Royal Hospital, Chelsea 76, *80*
    St James's Park *80*, *81*
    St Pancras Station 75
    St Paul's Cathedral 76, *77*, 79
    Tower of London 74, 76, 78
    Westminster Hall 77
    Whitehall *81*
Longleat *62-3*
Ludlow 119
Lygon family 92, 98
Lyme Regis 49, *50*

Macbeth 150
McCaig's folly, Oban *156*
Madresfield Court 92, *98-9*
Marlowe, Christopher 84, 86, 93
Mary, Queen of Scots 118-19, 150-1, 154
May, Walter Barton 34
Mentmore Towers *110*
Monck, General 158
Monmouth, Duke of 49, 51, 64, 72
More, Sir Thomas 77, 78
Mortimer, Roger 90, 94, 118

Nash, John 100
Nelson, Lord *1*, 46, 48, 79, 85
Newton, Sir Isaac 84, 86, 118
Nicolson, Harold 16
Norman Conquest 12-14, 83, 126, 148

Norwich 85
Nottingham 118
Nunney Castle *61*

Oban *156*
Offa's Dyke 119, 126, 129
Osborne House *52-3*

Paxton, Sir Joseph 110
Pembroke Castle 128, *136-7*
Penshurst Place 15, *44-5*
Pevensey Bay 12
Pilgrim Fathers 48, 66
Plymouth 46-8, *66-7*
Portchester Castle 60
Portmeirion 129, *134-5*
Portsmouth *1*, 46, *60*
Prideaux, Sir Edmund 64

Ralegh, Sir Walter 46, 49, 66, 68
Repton, Humphrey 92
Richard II 23, 128
Richard III 116, 126, 138, 142
Robert the Bruce 150, 153
Romans 12, 60, 74-6, 82, 119, 126, 138, 148, 150
Rothschild, Meyer de 110
Roxburgh, Dukes of 155
Royal Navy 46, 66
Rye 15, 17, *18-19*, 26

Sackville family 41
Sackville-West, Vita 16, 41
Saffron Walden 84, 89
St Andrew's *156*
St Michael's Mount 59
Salisbury Cathedral 73
Saxons 60, 102
Scotney Castle 14-15, *17*
Scott, Sir George Gilbert 75
Sezincote 92, *101*
Shakespeare, William 93, 103, 116, 150
Sherborne 68-9
Shrewbury 119
Sidney, Sir Philip 44, 119
Sissinghurst Castle *2*, 15, *16*
Spanish Armada 14, 48, 49, 51, 59, 66
Stephen, King 72, 124
Stevenson, Robert Louis 48
Stirling Bridge, battle of

149
Stirling Castle 149, *159*
Stonehenge 47
Stourhead *70*
Stratfield Saye *111*
Stratford-on-Avon *91*, 93, *103*

Taunton *72*
Telford, Thomas 97
Thorpeness 85
Tintern Abbey *132-3*
Trafalgar, battle of *1*, 46
Trollope, Anthony 73
Tunbridge Wells *42-3*

Urquhart Castle *157*

Vanbrugh, Sir John 140
Victoria, Queen 30, 52, 111
Victory, HMS *1*, 46
Vikings 12, 82, 102, 138, 145, 146

Wallace, Sir William 149, 150
Wallace Monument *149*
Wars of the Roses 102, 116, 118, 125, 127, 128
Warwick Castle *102*
Washington, Co. Durham 141
Waugh, Evelyn 92, 98
Wellington, Duke of 77, 79, 111
West Indies, exiles in 51
West Wycombe Park 104-6, *112-13*
Wilkinson, John 9
William the Conqueror 12-14, 24, 49, 76, 78, 82, 118, *125*, 126, 148
William of Orange 66, Williams-Ellis, Sir Clough 129, 134
Winchelsea 17, 26
Winchester 49
Windsor Castle 131
Woburn Abbey *114-15*
Woolf, Virginia 41
Wordsworth, William 132, 140
Wren, Sir Christopher 76, 79, 80
Wyatt, James 125

York 138-40, *143*